Borland® Pascal
with Objects

Version 7.0

User's Guide

BORLAND INTERNATIONAL, INC.   1800 GREEN HILLS ROAD
P.O. BOX 660001, SCOTTS VALLEY, CA 95067-0001

R1   10 9 8 7 6 5 4 3 2 1

C O N T E N T S

T A B L E S

F I G U R E S

L I S T I N G S

Borland Pascal with Objects is designed for all types of users who want to develop applications for the DOS operating system or the Windows operating environment. You can create DOS real-mode, Windows, or DOS protected-mode applications in either a DOS or Windows environment. Borland Pascal offers a rich programming environment that makes software development more productive —and more fun. Using Pascal's structured, high-level language, you can write programs for any type or size of application.

Borland Pascal 7.0 brings you new capabilities while remaining compatible with code written for Turbo Pascal or Turbo Pascal for Windows. While exploring the opportunities that await you, remember that this is still the quick and efficient Pascal compiler that is the world's standard.

How to use the Borland Pascal manuals

Borland Pascal comes with eleven manuals, each with a different purpose.

Read the User's Guide if you've never used Turbo Pascal before.

You'll find the *User's Guide* helpful if

- You want to know how to install Borland Pascal
- You've used Turbo Pascal or Turbo Pascal for Windows before and you want to know what is new in this release
- You want to learn how to use Borland's integrated development environment (the IDE) to develop and debug programs
- You want to learn about units and how to write your own
- You haven't used pointers in your programs before or you need to refresh your pointer knowledge
- You're new to object-oriented programming
- You want an introduction to ObjectWindows

Read the Language Guide to learn about the Borland Pascal language.

The *Language Guide* focuses on the Borland Pascal language and explains how to get the most out of it. Use the *Language Guide* to

- Find the formal definition of the Borland Pascal language including detailed syntax diagrams covering every Borland Pascal construct
- Learn how to use dynamic-link libraries and how to write your own
- Learn how the run-time libraries are organized and how to use them
- Discover the procedures, functions, predeclared variables, constants, and so on that are in the run-time libraries and available for your programs to use
- Find out how Borland Pascal programs use memory
- Learn how Borland Pascal implements program control
- Learn how Borland Pascal optimizes code
- Find out how to use Borland Pascal with assembly language

Use the Programmer's Reference as your primary reference when programming in Borland Pascal.

The *Programmer's Reference* is a reference to all the details you'll need. Keep this volume by your computer as you program. Use the *Programmer's Reference* when you want to

- Look up the details of a particular run-time library procedure, function, variable, type, or constant and find out how to use it
- Understand how compiler directives work, what each compiler directive does, and how to use them
- Find out what an error message means
- Learn how to use the command-line compiler
- Look up editor commands
- Look up compiler directives in a quick reference
- See a list of reserved words and standard directives

Use the Turbo Vision Programming Guide to learn about developing for DOS with Turbo Vision.

The *Turbo Vision Programming Guide* introduces you to and explains Turbo Vision, the application framework that gives you a head start on DOS object-oriented programming. To master Turbo Vision, you'll want to

- Work through the tutorial to get hands-on experience developing a Turbo Vision application
- Study the Turbo Vision hierarchy and become acquainted with the object types

- Learn the meaning of event-driven programming and what it entails
- Use the Turbo Vision reference to look up the details about the objects in the Turbo Vision hierarchy and all the associated types, constants, and variables

Use the ObjectWindows Programming Guide to learn about programming for Windows with Object-Windows.

The *ObjectWindows Programming Guide* is your guide to developing true Windows applications with Borland Pascal's Object-Windows library. To master ObjectWindows, you'll want to

- Work through the tutorial to get hands-on experience developing an ObjectWindows application
- Study the ObjectWindows hierarchy, then read further to understand the tasks you can perform on ObjectWindows objects
- Learn how to manage graphics, resources, and data in your ObjectWindows programs
- Use the ObjectWindows reference to look up all the details about all the objects in the ObjectWindows hierarchy and all the associated types, constants, and variables

Use the Tools and Utilities Guide to learn about the tools that can make programming with Borland Pascal even more productive.

The *Tools and Utilities Guide* explains how to use the tools and utilities that come with Borland Pascal. Refer to the *Tools and Utilities Guide* if you want to

- Learn how to use TPUMOVER to add and delete units to the Borland Pascal run-time library.
- Find out how to use MAKE, the project manager.
- Use WinSight to examine the messages your Windows application receives and dispatches.
- Use WinSpector to inspect your Windows application after it receives an Unrecoverable Application Error to help you determine what went wrong.
- Read about using the Resource Compiler for compiling your Windows resources. You'll no doubt prefer to use Borland's Resource Workshop to create resources, but we include the Resource Compiler for completeness.
- Learn how to create Windows 3.0 and 3.1 Help files.
- Find out how to use the memory resident Borland Pascal help system, Turbo Help, when working with command-line tools.

In addition to these Borland Pascal-specific books, the Borland Pascal package includes the following books that can be used with Borland Pascal and other Borland language products:

- *Turbo Debugger User's Guide*
- *Turbo Profiler User's Guide*
- *Resource Workshop User's Guide*
- *Turbo Assembler User's Guide*
- *Turbo Assembler Quick Reference*

Typefaces used in these books

All typefaces used in this manual were produced by Borland's Sprint: The Professional Word Processor, on a PostScript laser printer. Their uses are as follows:

`Monospace type` — This typeface represents text as it appears on-screen or in a program. It is also used for anything you must type (such as `BP` to start up Borland Pascal).

`[ ]` — Square brackets in text or DOS command lines enclose optional items that depend on your system. *Text of this sort should not be typed verbatim.*

Boldface — This typeface is used in text for Borland Pascal reserved words, for compiler directives {$I-}, and for command-line options (/**A**).

Italics — Italics indicate identifiers that appear in text. They can represent terms that you can use as they are, or that you can think up new names for (your choice, usually). They are also used to emphasize certain words, such as new terms.

Keycaps — This typeface indicates a key on your keyboard. For example, "Press *Esc* to exit a menu."

This icon indicates keyboard actions.

This icon indicates mouse actions.

How to contact Borland

Borland offers a variety of services to answer your questions about Borland Pascal.

 Be sure to send in the registration card; registered owners are entitled to technical support and may receive information on upgrades and supplementary products.

TechFax

800-822-4269 (voice)

TechFax is a 24-hour automated service that sends free technical information to your fax machine. You can use your touch-tone phone to request up to three documents per call.

Borland Download BBS

408-439-9096 (modem)
up to 9600 Baud

The Borland Download BBS has sample files, applications, and technical information you can download with your modem. No special setup is required.

Online information services

Subscribers to the CompuServe, GEnie, or BIX information services can receive technical support by modem. Use the commands in the following table to contact Borland while accessing an information service.

Online information services

Service	Command
CompuServe	GO BORLAND
BIX	JOIN BORLAND
GEnie	BORLAND

Address electronic messages to Sysop or All. Don't include your serial number; messages are in public view unless sent by a service's private mail system. Include as much information on the question as possible; the support staff will reply to the message within one working day.

Borland Technical Support

408-461-9177 (Pascal)
6 a.m. to 5 p.m. PT

Borland Technical Support is available weekdays from 6:00 a.m. to 5:00 p.m. Pacific Time to answer technical questions about

Borland products. Please call from a telephone near your computer, with the program running and the following information available:

- Product name, serial number, and version number
- Brand and model of the hardware in your system
- Operating system and version number—use the operating system's VER command to find the version number
- Contents of your AUTOEXEC.BAT and CONFIG.SYS files (located in the root directory (\) of your computer's boot disk)
- Contents of your WIN.INI and SYSTEM.INI files (located in your Windows directory)
- Windows version number—use the WINVER command to find the versions number
- Daytime phone number where you can be reached

If the call concerns a software problem, please be able to describe the steps that will reproduce the problem.

Borland Technical Support also publishes technical information sheets on a variety of topics.

Borland Advisor Line

900-555-1001
6 a.m. to 5 p.m. PT
The Borland Advisor Line is a service for users who need immediate access to advice on Borland Pascal issues.

The Advisor Line operates weekdays from 6:00 a.m. to 5:00 p.m. Pacific Time. The first minute is free; each subsequent minute is $2.00.

Borland Customer Service

408-461-9000 (voice)
7 a.m. to 5 p.m. PT
Borland Customer Service is available weekdays from 7:00 a.m. to 5:00 p.m. Pacific time to answer nontechnical questions about Borland products, including pricing information, upgrades, and order status.

1

Installing and running Borland Pascal

Your Borland Pascal package includes five different versions of Borland Pascal:

- BP.EXE, an integrated development environment (IDE) that runs in DOS protected mode and generates DOS real-mode, Windows, or DOS protected-mode applications
- BPW.EXE, an IDE that runs under Windows and generates DOS real-mode, Windows, or DOS protected-mode applications
- TURBO.EXE, an IDE that runs in DOS real mode and generates DOS real-mode applications only
- BPC.EXE, a command-line compiler that runs in DOS protected mode and generates DOS real-mode, Windows, or DOS protected-mode applications
- TPC.EXE, a command-line compiler that runs in DOS real mode and generates DOS real-mode applications only

Borland Pascal comes with an automatic installation program called INSTALL. Because we use file-compression techniques, you must use this program; you can't just copy the Borland Pascal files onto your hard disk. INSTALL automatically copies and uncompresses the Borland Pascal and Borland Pascal for Windows files.

We assume you're already familiar with DOS commands. For example, you'll need the DISKCOPY command to make backup copies of your distribution disks (the disks you bought). Make a complete working copy of your distribution disks when you receive them, then store the original disks away in a safe place.

This chapter contains the following information:

- Installing Borland Pascal and Borland Pascal for Windows on your system
- Accessing the README file
- Accessing the HELPME!.DOC file
- Using Borland's example programs

Using INSTALL

Among other things, INSTALL detects what hardware you're using and configures Borland Pascal appropriately. It also creates directories as needed and transfers files from your distribution disks to your hard disk. Its actions are self-explanatory; the following text tells you all you need to know.

To install Borland Pascal,

1. Insert the installation disk (disk 1) into drive A. Type the following command, then press *Enter*:

   ```
   A:INSTALL
   ```

2. Press *Enter* at the installation screen.

3. Follow the prompts.

4. INSTALL needs disk space to store temporary files before decompressing them. INSTALL's opening screen lists the disk-space requirements; if you don't have enough, exit INSTALL and make room. Once INSTALL is complete, those temporary files are deleted.

5. At the end of installation, you might want to add this line to your CONFIG.SYS file:

   ```
   FILES = 20
   ```

If you changed the default installation directory, you need to change this PATH setting.

and this line to your AUTOEXEC.BAT file (or modify your existing PATH statement, if you already have one):

```
PATH = C:\BP\BIN
```

When INSTALL is finished, it allows you to read the latest about Borland Pascal in the README file, which contains important last-minute information.

INSTALL and Windows

The next time you start Microsoft Windows (after you exit from the README file viewer), you'll be asked if you want to create a Borland Pascal program group in Program Manager. If you choose Yes, Windows creates the program group, which contains icons for the Borland Pascal and Borland Pascal for Windows programs and utilities.

 INSTALL assumes that Windows is installed in the directory you specified as your Windows directory during installation. It also assumes that the Program Manager starts up automatically as your Windows "shell" when you start Windows. If you normally use a different command shell from Program Manager, you might need to edit the SYSTEM.INI file in your Windows directory to include this line:

```
SHELL=PROGMAN.EXE
```

Otherwise you'll get a message saying "cannot communicate with Program Manager" when you first open Windows and Borland Pascal tries to create a new Program Manager group. Once Borland Pascal for Windows and the other tools are installed in a Program Manager group, you can examine their settings, then reinstall them in your alternate command shell if you want.

Running Borland Pascal

For information about starting the Windows IDE, see page 11. To start Borland Pascal, go to the Borland Pascal BIN directory created with INSTALL. Usually this directory is C:\BP\BIN. To start the protected-mode IDE, type

```
BP
```

 The files DPMI16BI.OVL and RTM.EXE must be in your current directory or on your path or BP.EXE won't start.

To start the IDE that runs in real mode, type

```
TURBO
```

Protected mode and memory

The DOS protected-mode IDE, the command-line compiler, and other protected-mode tools use DPMI (DOS Protected Mode Interface) to run the compiler in protected mode, giving you access to all your computer's memory. In addition, you can use Borland Pascal to write your own protected-mode applications. The protected-mode interface is completely transparent to the user, and you should never have to think about it, with a few possible exceptions.

DPMIINST
One such exception might be when you run Borland Pascal for the very first time. Borland Pascal uses an internal database of various machine characteristics to determine how to enable protected mode on your machine, and configures itself accordingly. If you have a computer with an older 80286 microprocessor, Borland Pascal might not recognize your machine. You'll see this message when you try to run Borland Pascal:

```
Machine not in database (RUN DPMIINST)
```

If you get this message, simply run the DPMIINST program by typing DPMIINST at the DOS prompt and following the program's instructions.

DPMIINST runs your machine through a series of tests to determine the best way of enabling protected mode, and automatically configures Borland Pascal accordingly. Once you have run DPMIINST, you won't have to run it again.

 Some memory managers, device drivers, and memory-resident (TSR) programs can interfere with DPMIINST's ability to analyze your machine. If DPMIINST fails, try temporarily disabling or removing these programs. That gives DPMIINST the unrestricted access it needs to determine the best way to enter protected mode.

DPMIMEM
By default, the Borland Pascal DPMI interface allocates all available extended and expanded memory for its own use. If you don't want all of the available memory to be taken by the DPMI kernel, you can set an environment variable to specify the maximum amount of memory to use. This variable can be entered directly at the DOS prompt or inserted as a line in your AUTOEXEC.BAT file, using this syntax:

```
SET DPMIMEM=MAXMEM nnnn
```

where *nnnn* is the amount of memory in kilobytes.

For example, if you have a system with 4MB and want the DPMI kernel to use 2MB of it, leaving the other 2MB alone, the DPMIMEM variable would be set as follows:

```
SET DPMIMEM=MAXMEM 2000
```

RTMRES

RTMRES preloads the DPMI server. It enables DPMI and spawns a DOS command shell. Preloading the DPMI server lets you load Borland Pascal's protected-mode tools such as BP, BPC, TASMX, and so on slightly faster. Type EXIT to close the shell.

RTMRES is especially useful if you use BPC, the command-line compiler that runs in DOS protected mode. Every time you invoke it, the DPMI server is loaded. If you've run RTMRES previously, the server is already present, and the command-line compiler loads faster.

Borland Pascal and extended memory

Once the DPMI kernel is loaded (either by running BP or with the RTMRES utility), the Borland Pascal IDE interacts with the DPMI server through Borland's run-time manager (RTM.EXE) to allocate memory so that the IDE can load and operate. By default, the IDE uses all the extended memory reserved by the DPMI kernel.

Running Borland Pascal from Windows

To run Borland Pascal for Windows, click the Borland Pascal for Windows icon in the Program Manager. You can also run the two DOS IDEs from Windows; you'll find icons for each of these in the Program Manager.

Running BP.EXE in Windows 386 enhanced mode

The DOS protected-mode IDE should run just fine if you run Windows in 386 enhanced mode. You won't need to set the DPMIMEM variable; instead use the Borland Pascal PIF file for Windows (BP\BIN\BP.PIF) to configure the amount of memory available to Borland Pascal if you wish.

Running BP.EXE in Windows standard mode

Preloading the DPMI server lets you run the protected-mode tools (BP, BPC, TASMX and so on) in Windows standard-mode DOS windows. Do this by running RTMRES.EXE as described earlier on page 11. When using RTMRES in conjunction with Windows, always set the DPMIMEM variable to less than the maximum available memory to insure that Windows has enough physical memory to operate.

 If you are running under a RTMRES shell, you can't run Windows in 386 enhanced mode, because the DPMI server, by default, allocates all extended memory for its own use, leaving none for Windows. You must first exit the shell and then run Windows, or use the DPMIMEM variable to restrict the amount of memory the DPMI server allocates.

Running BP.EXE in a Windows DOS box

If you choose to start the protected-mode IDE in a Windows DOS box, you must first modify the DOSPRMPT.PIF file found in your Windows directory so that the protected-mode IDE will be able to use extended memory.

Using the PIF editor, open the DOSPRMPT.PIF file, and indicate the amount of extended memory you want the protected-mode IDE to use. If you are unsure how to use the PIF editor, see your *Microsoft Windows User's Guide*.

LCD and plasma screens

If you have a computer with an LCD or plasma display, you should start Borland Pascal using the /L startup option. Type this:

```
BP /L
```

or

```
TURBO /L
```

Although you could always start Borland Pascal this way, you can also easily configure the IDE for a black-and-white screen from within the IDE, using the Options | Environment | Startup dialog box. Choose the LCD Color Set option.

The README file

The README file contains last-minute information that might not be in the manuals.

Borland Pascal automatically places you in the README file when you run the INSTALL program. To access the README file at a later time, you can use the Borland Pascal README program by typing these commands at the DOS command line:

```
CD \BP
README
```

FILELIST.DOC and HELPME!.DOC

Your installation disk also contains a file called FILELIST.DOC, which lists every file on the distribution disks and a brief description of what each one contains, and HELPME!.DOC, which contains answers to problems that users commonly run into. Consult HELPME!.DOC if you have difficulties. You can use the README program to look at FILELIST.DOC or HELPME!.DOC. Type this at the command line:

```
README HELPME!.DOC
```

or

```
README FILELIST.DOC
```

Example programs

Your Borland Pascal package includes the source code for a large number of example programs for both DOS and Windows. These programs are located in subdirectories of the EXAMPLES directory created by INSTALL. The EXAMPLES directory also contains subdirectories for examples of the other tools and utilities that come with Borland Pascal (such as Turbo Assembler, Turbo Debugger, and Resource Workshop). Spend a few moments browsing through these directories to see the wealth of program examples available to you.

2

What's new in Borland Pascal

Borland Pascal with Objects is a professional object-oriented programming system for DOS real mode, DOS protected mode, and Windows. If you are a Turbo Pascal or Turbo Pascal for Windows user, this chapter tells you about all the new features in Borland Pascal and where you can find information about them.

Three integrated development environments

Borland Pascal gives you three integrated development environments (IDEs):

You must have a 80286 or higher microprocessor in your computer and at least 2MB of memory to run the DOS protected-mode IDE.

- BP.EXE, a DOS IDE that runs in DOS protected mode and creates your choice of DOS real-mode, Windows, or DOS protected-mode applications. A protected-mode IDE means even your very large applications will have the memory necessary to compile.

- BPW.EXE, a Windows IDE that creates your choice of DOS real-mode, Windows, or DOS protected-mode applications.

- TURBO.EXE, a DOS real-mode IDE that creates DOS real-mode applications only and runs on all 80x86 systems.

To read about the DOS IDEs, see Chapter 4, "Programming in a DOS IDE," in this book. To read about features specific to the Windows IDE, see Chapter 5, "Programming in the Windows IDE."

New IDE features

Within these IDEs, you'll find these new features:

- Two ObjectBrowsers, one in the DOS protected-mode IDE and one in the Windows IDE. With the ObjectBrowsers, you can browse through the objects and units in your program, examine your source code, obtain a complete cross-reference to every symbol used in your program, and see your program in a new perspective. To read about the DOS ObjectBrowser, see page 64 in this book. To read about the Windows ObjectBrowser, see page 96.

- Syntax highlighting. Within all the IDEs, you can color code syntax elements of your programs so you can quickly identify parts of your code. In the Windows IDE, you can also boldface, italicize, or underline syntax elements. In all the IDEs, you can print syntax-highlighted code. To learn how to use syntax highlighting, see page 49 in Chapter 4, "Programming in a DOS IDE," and page 91 in Chapter 5, "Programming in the Windows IDE."

- A SpeedBar in the Windows IDE. The SpeedBar is a quick way to choose menu commands and other actions with a mouse. You can choose to display it horizontally, vertically, or as a floating palette—or even turn it off completely. Read about the SpeedBar on page 84 in this book.

- Undo and Redo in both the DOS and Windows editors. Make a mistake while editing your program? Press Undo and your mistake disappears. Press Redo, and it reappears. For more about Undo and Redo, see page 44 in this book.

- A Tools menu. You can run the tools and utilities that come with Borland Pascal directly from the IDE. In the DOS IDEs, you can also add your own utilities to the Tools menu and change the hot keys to your liking. To learn about the Tools menu in the DOS IDEs, see page 75 in this book. For the Tools menu in the Windows IDE, see page 103.

- A Messages window in the DOS IDEs. You can use the Messages window to display output messages from utilities such as GREP. You can choose to edit a program line referenced in a message, or track messages in your source code as you scroll through the messages. To learn about the Messages window, see page 77 in this book.

16

- Local menus in all IDEs. With just a click of your right mouse button or by pressing *Alt+F10*, you can display a local menu that lists menu commands specific to the active window. Read about local menus on page 49 in this book.

- Symbol information saved across sessions. This enables you to browse, debug, or run your program without recompiling after you have exited and then restarted the IDE; see page 80 in this book.

- Symbol information saved across compilations. If you compile a program successfully, modify your source code and recompile, and your compilation fails, you can still use the symbol information from your last successful compilation to browse and perhaps find the source of your problem. See page 65 in this book.

- Multiple user-installable Help file support in the DOS IDEs. You can load additional Help files into the Borland Pascal Help system. The IDE merges the indexes of the newly-loaded Help files with the standard Help system index. For more information about loading new help files, see page 42 in this book.

A protected-mode command-line compiler

BPC.EXE, a command-line compiler, runs in protected mode, so even very large programs have sufficient memory to compile successfully. Like the DOS protected-mode IDE, BPC.EXE can create DOS real-mode, Windows, and DOS protected-mode applications. Read about the command-line compiler in Chapter 3, "Command-line compilers," in the *Programmer's Reference*.

DOS protected-mode application development

With the BP.EXE IDE and the BPC.EXE command-line compiler, you can create programs that run in DOS protected mode without the need for overlays. Your programs can finally exceed the DOS real-mode 640K barrier.

For many of your programs, all you have to do to create a DOS protected-mode application is select DOS protected mode as your target platform and set the appropriate compiler options; pages 54 and 57 in this book tell you how. But you'll also want to read Chapter 17, "Programming in DOS protected mode," in the *Language Guide*, which explains protected-mode issues in depth.

DOS dynamic-link libraries

Dynamic-link libraries (DLLs) have traditionally been a part of Windows program development. With Borland Pascal, you can also create DOS DLLs.

DLLs are loaded at run time, are separate from your .EXEs, and can be shared between multiple applications. DOS DLLs run in DOS protected mode and are fully compatible with Windows DLLs, enabling you to share DLLs between your DOS and Windows applications. To read about dynamic-link libraries, see Chapter 11, "Dynamic-link libraries," in the *Language Guide*.

Additions to the Pascal language

Borland Pascal has several new language extensions that make writing your programs easier:

- Open parameters. Open parameters allow strings and arrays of varying sizes to be passed to a procedure or function. Read about open parameters in the "Open parameters" section on page 113 in Chapter 9, "Procedures and functions," in the *Language Guide*.

- **Public** standard directive. Turbo Pascal 6.0 and Turbo Pascal for Windows permitted **private** component sections in objects. Borland Pascal introduces **public** component sections that have no restrictions on the scope of fields and methods declared in them. You can mix **public** and **private** component sections in your objects as you see fit. To read more about the new **public** standard directive, see the "Components and scope" section on page 36 in Chapter 4, "Types," in the *Language Guide*.

- **Inherited** reserved word. The **inherited** reserved word can be used within a method to refer to the ancestor of the method's object type. See the "Qualified-method activations" section on page 41 in Chapter 4, "Types," in the *Language Guide*.

- Constant parameters. Procedures and functions can list constant parameters: a parameter group preceded by the **const** reserved word and followed by a type. Constant parameters protect against accidental assignments to a formal parameter, and in some cases, permit the compiler to generate more efficient code. See the "Parameters" section on page 109 in Chapter 9, "Procedures and functions," in the *Language Guide*.

■ Dynamic methods and dynamic method tables (DMTs). If you've used Turbo Pascal for Windows, you know about dynamic methods and DMTs. With Borland Pascal, your DOS programs can use them too.

Dynamic methods differ from virtual methods in the way dynamic methods are dispatched at run time. Instead of building a virtual method table (VMT) for dynamic methods, the compiler builds a DMT. Usually DMTs decrease the memory requirements of your applications when you program with objects. To learn more about dynamic methods, see the "Dynamic methods" section on page 38 in Chapter 4, "Types," in the *Language Guide*. To read more about dynamic method tables, see the "Dynamic method tables" section on page 283 in Chapter 21, "Memory issues," in the *Language Guide*.

Enhancements to the run-time library

Borland Pascal has three run-time libraries: TURBO.TPL for DOS real-mode programs, TPW.TPL for Windows programs, and TPP.TPL for DOS protected-mode programs.

Improvements to the run-time libraries include these items:

■ Quicker text-file input and output

■ A faster *Pos* function

■ 80386 optimizations for *Longint* multiply, divide, shift left, and shift right operations

New routines in the System unit

The *System* unit has seven new procedures and functions. You can find them all in Chapter 1, "Library reference," in the *Programmer's Reference*:

■ The *Assigned* procedure tests to determine if a pointer or procedural variable is **nil**.

- The *Break* procedure terminates a **for**, **while**, or **repeat** statement.
- The *Continue* procedure continues with the next iteration of a **for**, **while**, or **repeat** statement.
- The *Include* procedure includes an element in a set.
- The *Exclude* procedure excludes an element in a set.
- The *High* function returns the highest value in the range of the argument.
- The *Low* function returns the lowest value in the range of the argument.

New units

With the *Strings* unit, Turbo Pascal for Windows programmers could use null-terminated (C-style) strings. Now both DOS and Windows programmers can use the *Strings* unit. To learn more null-terminated strings, see Chapter 18, "Using null-terminated strings," in the *Language Guide*. For complete information about all the procedures and functions in the *Strings* unit, see Chapter 1, "Library reference," in the *Programmer's Reference*.

Turbo Pascal for Windows programmers are already familiar with the *WinDos* unit. DOS programmers can also use the *WinDos* unit to implement operating system and file-handling routines. To help you decide if you should use the *WinDos* or the *Dos* unit, read Chapter 16, "Interfacing with DOS," in the *Language Guide*. All *WinDos* procedures and functions are explained in detail in Chapter 1, "Library reference," in the *Programmer's Reference*.

The *WinAPI* unit gives you direct access to Borland's protected-mode DOS extensions. The *WinAPI* interface is designed as a subset of the Windows API to make it easier to write portable applications and binary-compatible DLLs. To learn about *WinAPI*, read the "WinAPI unit" section on page 203 in Chapter 17, "Programming in DOS protected mode," in the *Language Guide*. For complete information about the *WinAPI* procedures and functions, see Chapter 1, "Library reference," in the *Programmer's Reference*.

The *WinPrn* unit allows you to send the output of your Windows program to the printer of your choice. Read about printing in a Windows program on page 170 in Chapter 14, "Input and output," in the *Language Guide*, and look up expanded explanations of the *WinPrn* procedures and functions in Chapter 1, "Library reference," in the *Programmer's Reference*.

The *Win31* unit provides an interface to the additional API routines found in the Windows 3.1 KERNEL and USER DLLs. Applications that use the *Win31* unit don't run under Windows 3.0. For more information about the *Win31* unit, use the Borland Pascal Help system.

Borland Pascal supports the remaining extensions to the Windows 3.1 API in several units; you can find information about them in the Borland Pascal Help system:

ColorDlg	*LZExpand*	*ShellAPI*
CommDlg	*MMSystem*	*Stress*
Cpl	*OLE*	*ToolHelp*
DDEML	*PenWin*	*Ver*
Dlgs	*Print*	*WinMem32*

New compiler directives

Borland Pascal has five new compiler directives; read more about them in Chapter 2, "Compiler directives," in the *Programmer's Reference*:

- The **$P** directive, Open String Parameters, controls the meaning of variable parameters declared using the **string** keyword.
- The **$T** directive, Type-checked Pointers, controls the types of pointer values generated by the @ operator.
- The **$Q** directive, Overflow Checking, controls the generation of overflow-checking code for certain integer arithmetic operations.
- The **$K** directive, Smart Callbacks, controls the generation of smart callbacks for procedures and functions that are exported by a Windows application. For more details about how Borland Pascal handles smart callbacks, see "Entry and exit code" on page 298 in Chapter 22, "Control issues," in the *Language Guide*.
- The **$Y** directive, Symbol Information, generates symbol reference information in a compiled program or unit so that the ObjectBrowser can display symbol definition and reference information for that module.

Improvements to the compiler

In addition to the extensions to the Borland Pascal language and the new compiler directives, the compiler itself continues to improve:

- The compiler permits easier linking with C and assembler code by passing .OBJ line number information to your executable file. Therefore, you can use the integrated debugger to step through C and assembler code; see page 113 in Chapter 6, "Debugging in the IDE," in this book.
- The compiler generates more efficient code when the right operand of the **in** operator is a set constant. See "Constant set inlining" on page 307 in Chapter 23, "Optimizing your code," in the *Language Guide*.
- The compiler generates more efficient code for small sets. To read about small sets, see page 308 in Chapter 23, "Optimizing your code," in the *Language Guide*.
- The compiler permits unlimited unit nesting.
- A **uses** clause in the **implementation** section of a unit no longer causes a circular unit reference.
- The compiler suppresses redundant pointer load operations in certain situations; see Chapter 23, "Optimizing your code," in the *Language Guide*.

Enhancements to Turbo Vision

Turbo Vision 2.0 adds new objects to the hierarchy and adds some new capabilities to the existing objects. Changes to existing objects are backward-compatible, so existing Turbo Vision code should compile without changes, and existing streams and resources should load without error.

These are the new features in Turbo Vision 2.0; read about them in the *Turbo Vision Programming Guide*:

- Support for data validation. Your Turbo Vision applications can ensure that they receive valid data to process.
- Multistate check boxes. Check boxes can have states other than checked and unchecked. The DOS protected-mode IDE

(BP.EXE) uses multi-state check boxes in its Compiler Options dialog box.

- Outline viewer objects. Your applications can use two objects, *TOutlineViewer* and *TOutline,* to display outlines. The DOS ObjectBrowser uses these objects.

- Object versioning on a stream. Even if your objects were created with Turbo Vision 1.0, your programs will still be able to read them as objects compatible with Turbo Vision 2.0.

- New tutorial and revised documentation. You'll find it easier to learn Turbo Vision and to become proficient quickly.

Enhancements to ObjectWindows

ObjectWindows adds new objects to the hierarchy and some new capabilities to the existing objects.

The *WObjects* unit no longer exists. Your existing code will recompile successfully if you replace every reference to the *WObjects* unit with the *OWindows, ODialogs, OMemory* and *Objects* units.

These are the new features in ObjectWindows; read about them in the *ObjectWindows Programming Guide:*

- Support for data validation. Your ObjectWindows applications can ensure that they receive valid data to process.

- Printing objects. Printing in an ObjectWindows program is easier with the new printing objects.

- Support for Borland Windows Custom Controls. Your Object-Windows programs can have the Borland look.

New tools and utilities

If Windows is your target platform, you have two new tools to aid your development process; read about them in the *Tools and Utilities Guide:*

- WinSight. WinSight is a debugging tool that gives you information about windows, window classes, and messages. Use it to study a Windows application—yours or others—to see how windows and window classes are created and used and what messages the windows receive as the program runs.

- WinSpector. With WinSpector, you can examine a Windows application after it crashes from an Unrecoverable Application Error (UAE) to help you understand why the crash happened.

Borland Pascal also includes updated versions of these tools:

- Turbo Debugger, including TDW, which can debug Windows applications, and TDX, which can debug DOS protected-mode applications.
- Turbo Profiler, which includes two profilers—one for DOS programs and one for Windows applications.
- Turbo Assembler, which can bring object-oriented programming to your assembly code.
- Resource Workshop, which runs in the Windows environment, can create all the resources (dialog boxes, cursors, bitmaps, icons, and so on) for your Windows applications.

3

DOS IDE basics

If you prefer using a command-line compiler, see Chapter 3, "Command-line compilers," in the Programmer's Reference.

Borland Pascal is more than just a fast, efficient Pascal compiler; it also features an easy-to-learn and easy-to-use integrated development environment (IDE). With Borland Pascal, you don't need to use a separate editor, compiler, linker, and debugger to create, debug, and run your Pascal programs. All these features are built into Borland Pascal, and they are all accessible from the IDE.

With the Borland Pascal package, you have a choice of three IDEs:

- BP.EXE, a DOS IDE that runs in protected mode and creates DOS real-mode, DOS protected-mode, and Windows applications.

  To run BP.EXE, you must have a computer with a 80286 or greater microprocessor and at least 2 megabytes of memory. Because this IDE runs in protected mode, its capacity is limited only by the amount of memory in your computer.

- TURBO.EXE, a DOS IDE that runs in real mode only and creates DOS real-mode applications only.

- BPW.EXE, a Windows IDE that creates Windows, DOS real-mode, and DOS protected-mode applications.

This chapter explains the basics of using either of the DOS IDEs.

If you're a Windows user, you already know the basics of the Windows IDE because you know how to use Windows itself. If you are new to Borland's Windows IDE, you should skim Chapter 4, "Programming in a DOS IDE," first. There are many similarities between the DOS and Windows IDEs; most tasks are

accomplished in the same manner in both. Once you have an understanding of how to perform programming tasks in an IDE, read Chapter 5, "Programming in the Windows IDE," to learn about features unique to the Windows IDE and how the Windows and DOS IDEs differ.

Starting the IDE

For information about Borland Pascal startup options, see page 36 in Chapter 4, "Programming in a DOS IDE."

Go to the Borland Pascal subdirectory you created with INSTALL. Usually this directory is C:\BP\BIN. To start the protected-mode IDE, enter this command:

    BP

 The files DPMI16BI.OVL and RTM.EXE must be in your current directory or on your path or BP.EXE won't start.

To start the IDE that runs in real mode, enter this command:

    TURBO

IDE components

There are three visible components to the IDE: the Menu bar at the top, the desktop, and the status line at the bottom.

The Menu bar and menus

The Menu bar is your primary access to all the menu commands. When the Menu bar is active, you'll see a highlighted menu title; this is the currently *selected* menu.

You can choose commands with either the keyboard or a mouse.

Here's how you choose menu commands using the keyboard:

1. Press *F10*. This activates the Menu bar.
2. Use the arrow keys to select the menu you want to display. Then press *Enter*.

To cancel an action, press Esc.

As a shortcut for this step, you can press the highlighted letter of the menu title. For example, from the Menu bar, press *E* to quickly display the Edit menu. Or, without activating the

User's Guide

Menu bar, you can press *Alt* and the highlighted letter to display the menu you want.

3. Use the arrow keys again to choose the menu command you want. Then press *Enter*.

Again, as a shortcut, you can just press the highlighted letter of a command to choose it once the menu is displayed.

At this point, Borland Pascal either carries out the command, displays a dialog box, or displays another menu.

You can customize the action of the Ctrl+right mouse button combination and even reverse the action of the mouse buttons; choose Options I Environment I Mouse.

To choose commands with a mouse, do this:

1. Click the desired menu title to display the menu.
2. Click the desired command.

You can also drag straight from the menu title down to the menu command. Release the mouse button on the command you want. If you change your mind, just drag off the menu; no command will be chosen.

If a menu command is followed by an ellipsis (...), choosing the command displays a dialog box. If the command is followed by an arrow (▶), the command leads to another menu (a pop-up menu). A command without either an ellipsis or an arrow indicates that the action occurs once you choose it.

At times menu commands will appear dim and, when you choose them, nothing happens. This occurs when choosing a particular command doesn't make sense in your current context. For example, if you don't have a block selected in your current edit window, you won't be able to cut, copy, or clear text because you haven't told the editor what text you want cut, copied, or cleared. The Cut, Copy, and Clear commands are therefore dimmed on the Edit menu. Once you select text in your edit window, you can choose these commands.

Shortcuts

From the keyboard, you can use a number of shortcuts (or *hot keys*) to access the Menu bar and choose commands. As you've already learned, you can get to, or activate, main menu items by pressing *Alt* and the highlighted letter. Once you're in a menu, you can press an item's highlighted letter or the hot key next to it. You can use a hot key from anywhere in the IDE—you don't have to display a menu first.

The status line also contains hot keys. Press the hot key or click the actual hot key representation on the status line to choose the associated command.

IDE windows

Most of what you see and do in the IDE happens in a *window*. A window is a screen area that you can move, resize, zoom, tile, overlap, close, and open.

Figure 3.1
A typical window

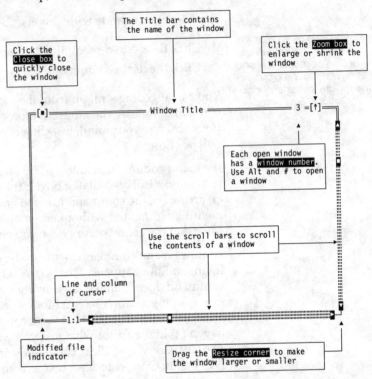

The Title bar contains the name of the window

Click the Close box to quickly close the window

Click the Zoom box to enlarge or shrink the window

Each open window has a window number. Use Alt and # to open a window

Use the scroll bars to scroll the contents of a window

Line and column of cursor

Modified file indicator

Drag the Resize corner to make the window larger or smaller

You can have many windows open in the IDE, but only one window can be *active* at any time. The active window is the one you're currently working in. Any command you choose or text you type generally applies only to the active window. If you have the same file open in several windows, any action to that file happens in all windows containing that file.

There are several types of windows, but most of them have these things in common:

- Title bar
- Close box
- Scroll bars
- Resize corner
- Zoom box
- A window number

The IDE makes it easy to spot the active window by placing a double-lined border partially around it. If your windows are overlapping, the active window is always the one on top of all the others (the frontmost one).

The active edit window displays the current line and column numbers in the lower left corner. If you've modified your file since you opened it or since you last saved it, an asterisk (∗) appears to the left of the column and line numbers.

The *Close box* of a window is the box in the upper left corner. You click this box to quickly close the window. Or choose Window | Close. The Help window and browser windows are considered temporary; you can close them by pressing *Esc*.

The *Title bar*, the topmost horizontal bar of a window, contains the name of the window and the window number. Double-clicking the Title bar zooms the window or restores it to its normal size if it is already enlarged. You can also drag the Title bar to move the window around.

Borland Pascal numbers only the first nine windows you open.

Each of the windows you open in the IDE has a *window number* in the upper-right border. *Alt+0* (zero) gives you a list of all the windows you have open. You can make a window active by pressing *Alt* in combination with the window number. For example, if the Help window is #5 but has gotten buried under the other windows, *Alt+5* brings it to the front.

Shortcut: Double-click the Title bar of a window to zoom or restore it.

The *Zoom box* of a window appears in the upper right corner. If the icon in that corner is an up arrow (↑), you can click the arrow to enlarge the window to the largest size possible. If the icon is a double-headed arrow (↕), the window is already at its maximum size. In that case, clicking it returns the window to its previous size. To zoom or restore a window from the keyboard, choose Window | Zoom, or press *F5*.

Scroll bars are horizontal or vertical bars. This is a horizontal scroll bar:

Scroll bars let you see how far into the file you've gone.

You use scroll bars with a mouse to scroll the contents of the window.

- To scroll one line at a time, click the arrow at either end.
- To scroll continuously, keep the mouse button pressed.
- To scroll one page at a time, click the shaded area to either side of the scroll box.
- To quickly move to a spot in the window relative to the position of the scroll box, drag the scroll box to any spot on the scroll bar.

The *Resize corner* is in the lower-right corner of a window. Drag the Resize corner to make the window larger or smaller. You can spot the Resize corner by its single-line border instead of the double-line border used in the rest of the window.

To resize a window using the keyboard, do this:

1. Choose Size/Move from the Window menu, or press *Ctrl+F5*.
2. Hold down the *Shift* key while you use the arrow keys to resize the window.

To move a window using the keyboard, do this:

1. Choose Size/Move from the Window menu, or press *Ctrl+F5*.
2. Use the arrow keys to resize the window.

Window management

Table 3.1 gives you a quick rundown of how to handle windows in Borland Pascal. You don't need a mouse to perform these actions—a keyboard works just fine.

Table 3.1
Manipulating windows

To accomplish this:	Use one of these methods:
Open an edit window	Choose File I Open to open a file and display it in a window, or press *F3*.
Open other windows	Choose the desired window from the Debug or Tools menu.
Close a window	Choose Window I Close, press *Alt+F3*, or click the Close box of the window.
See the previous window	Choose Window I Previous or press *Shift+F6*.
Activate a window	Click anywhere in the window, or

Table 3.1: Manipulating windows (continued)

	Press *Alt* plus the window number in the upper right border of the window), or
	Choose Window I List or press *Alt+0* and select the window from the list, or
	Choose Window I Next or *F6* to make the next window active (next in the order you first opened them). Or press *Shift+F6* to make your previous window active.
Move the active window	Drag its Title bar, or press *Ctrl+F5* (Window I Size/Move) and use the arrow keys to place the window where you want it, then press *Enter*.
Resize the active window	Drag the Resize corner (or any other corner). Or choose Window I Size/Move and press *Shift* while you use the arrow keys to resize the window, then press *Enter*. The shortcut is to press *Ctrl+F5* and then use *Shift* and the arrow keys.
Zoom the active window	Click the Zoom box in the upper right corner of the window, or
	Double-click the window's Title bar, or
	Choose Window I Zoom, or press *F5*.

The status line

The status line appears at the bottom of the screen. It has four purposes:

■ It reminds you of basic keystrokes and hot keys applicable at that moment in the active window.

■ It presents hot keys you can click to carry out the action instead of choosing the command from the menu or pressing the actual hot key.

■ It tells you what the program is doing. For example, it displays "Saving *filename...*" when you save a file in an edit window.

■ It offers one-line descriptions about any selected menu command and dialog-box items.

The status line changes as you switch windows or activities. One of the most common status lines is the one you see when you're writing and editing programs in an edit window. Here is what it looks like:

Figure 3.2
A typical status line

```
F1 Help    F2 Save    F3 Open    Alt+F9 Compile    F9 Make    F10 Menu
```

Dialog boxes

If a menu command has an ellipsis after it (...), the command opens a *dialog box*. A dialog box is a convenient way to view and set multiple options.

When you're selecting options in dialog boxes, you work with five basic types of onscreen controls: radio buttons, check boxes, action buttons, input boxes, and list boxes. Here's a typical dialog box that illustrates these items:

Figure 3.3
Typical dialog box

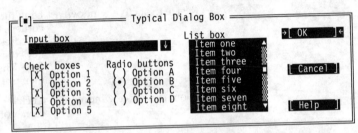

Action buttons

This dialog box has three standard action buttons: OK, Cancel, and Help.

■ If you choose OK, the choices in the dialog box are made in Borland Pascal.

■ If you choose Cancel, nothing changes and no action is done, but the dialog box is put away; the same thing happens if you click the Close box. *Esc* is always a keyboard shortcut for Cancel even if no Cancel button appears.

■ If you choose Help, the IDE opens a Help window about the dialog box.

If you're using a mouse, you can click the button you want. When you're using the keyboard, you can press the highlighted letter of an item to activate it. For example, pressing *K* selects the O**K** button. Press *Tab* or *Shift+Tab* to move forward or back respectively from one group to another in a dialog box, then use the ↑ and ↓ keys to select an item within the group. Each element is highlighted when it becomes active. When the button is selected, press *Enter* to choose it.

User's Guide

You can select another
button with Tab. Once a
button is selected, you press
Enter to choose the action of
the button.

In our typical dialog box, OK is the *default button*, which means you only need to press *Enter* to choose that button. (On monochrome systems, arrows indicate the default; on color monitors, default buttons are highlighted.) Be aware that selecting a button makes that button the default.

Check boxes and radio buttons

You can have any number of check boxes checked at any time. When you select a check box, an *X* appears in it to show you it's on. An empty box indicates it's off.

There are three ways to check a check box (set it to on):

- Click it or its text.
- Press *Tab* (and then the arrow keys) until the check box (or its group) is highlighted; press *Spacebar*.
- Type the highlighted letter in its text.

On monochrome monitors, the IDE indicates the active check box or group of check boxes by placing a chevron symbol (») next to it. When you press *Tab*, the chevron moves to the next group of check boxes or radio buttons.

Radio buttons act like the
old-style station-selection
buttons on a car radio. There
is always one—and only
one—button pushed in at a
time. Push one in, and the
one that was in pops out.

Radio buttons differ from check boxes in that they present mutually exclusive choices. For this reason, radio buttons *always* come in groups, and only one radio button can be on in any one group at any one time.

There are three ways to choose a radio button:

- Click it or its text.
- Type the highlighted letter in its associated text.
- Press *Tab* until the group is highlighted and then use the arrow keys to choose a particular radio button. Press *Tab* or *Shift+Tab* again to leave the group with the new radio button chosen.

Input boxes

An input box is where you enter text into the application. Most basic text-editing keys such as arrow keys, *Home, End,* and *Ins* work in the input box. If you continue to type once you reach the end of the box, the contents automatically scroll. If there's more text than what shows in the box, arrowheads appear at the end (◄ and ►). You can click the arrowheads to scroll the text.

If you need to enter control characters (such as ^L or ^M) in the input box, prefix the character with a ^P. For example, typing ^P^L enters a ^L into the input box. This is useful for search strings.

If an input box has a ↓ icon to its right, a *history list* is associated with that input box. Press ↓ or click the icon to view the history list and *Enter* to select an item from the list. The list displays any text you typed into the box the last few times you used it. If you want to re-enter text, press ↓ or click the ↓ icon. You can also edit an entry in the history list. Press *Esc* to exit from the history list without making a selection.

Here is what a history list for the Find input box might look like if you had used it several times previously:

Figure 3.4
Example of a history list in a
dialog box

List boxes

A final component of many dialog boxes is a *list box*. A list box lets you scroll through and select from variable-length lists without leaving a dialog box. If a blinking cursor appears in the list box and you know what you're looking for, you can begin typing the word or the first few letters of it, and the IDE searches the list for it.

You make a list box active by clicking it or by choosing the highlighted letter of the list title. You can also press *Tab* or the arrow keys until it's highlighted. Once a list box is displayed, you can use the scroll box to move through the list or press ↑ or ↓ from the keyboard.

Now that you know the fundamentals of using the IDE, you're ready to learn how to use the IDE to develop applications. See the next chapter, "Programming in a DOS IDE."

4

Programming in a DOS IDE

As you develop an application in the IDE, these are the major tasks you perform:

- Starting and exiting the IDE
- Writing and editing your source code
- Working with files (opening, closing, and saving them)
- Compiling and running your program
- Debugging your program
- Browsing through your source code
- Configuring the IDE to your preferences
- Managing your programming project

This chapter will give the basics on each of these topics, with the exception of debugging your program. Read Chapter 6, "Debugging in the IDE," to learn about debugging.

Starting and exiting

Go to the Borland Pascal subdirectory you created with INSTALL. Usually this directory is C:\BP\BIN. To start the protected-mode IDE, enter this command:

```
BP
```

The files DPMI16BI.OVL and RTM.EXE must be in your current directory or on your path, or BP.EXE won't start.

To start the IDE that runs in real mode, enter this command:

```
TURBO
```

You can use one or more options and file names along with the command to start the IDE.

Startup options

When you start the IDE, you can use startup options. The startup options use this syntax:

BP [/*options*] [*files*]

or

TURBO [/*options*] [*files*]

Placing a **+** or a space after the option turns it on. Placing a **–** after it turns it off. For example,

```
BP /G /P- myfile
```

starts up the IDE, opens an edit window with MYFILE in it, enables graphics memory save, and disables palette swapping.

You can also use a hyphen (**-**) before the option instead of a slash (/). For example,

```
BP -G -P- myfile
```

Some startup options apply only to the real-mode IDE, TURBO.EXE. You'll see the words "TURBO only" in the margin next to these. Two options apply only to the protected-mode IDE, BP.EXE; you'll see the words "BP only" in the margin.

The /C option

If you use the **/C** option followed by a configuration file name with no space in between, the IDE loads that configuration file when it starts. For example,

```
TURBO /Cmyconfig
```

For information about configuration files, see page 79.

The /D option

If you specify the **/D** option, the IDE can use dual monitors at the same time. The IDE checks whether your computer has the appropriate hardware, such as a monochrome card and a color card. If it doesn't, the IDE ignores this option. Dual-monitor mode is useful when debugging a program. You can see the program's output screen on one monitor and watch the debugger on the other. You can also shell to DOS (File | Shell to DOS) using two monitors so that one screen displays the IDE while the other gives you access to the DOS command line.

If your system has two monitors, DOS treats one monitor as the active monitor. Use the DOS MODE command to switch between the two monitors. For example, MODE CO80 activates the color monitor and MODE MONO activates the monochrome monitor. In dual-monitor mode, the normal IDE screen appears on the inactive monitor and program output goes to the active monitor.

So when you type BP /D or TURBO /D at the DOS prompt on one monitor, the IDE is displayed on the other monitor. When you want to test your program on a particular monitor, exit the IDE, switch the active monitor to the one you want to test with, and then issue the BP /D or TURBO /D command again. Program output will then go to the monitor where you typed the command.

☞ Keep the following in mind when using the /**D** option:

- Don't change the active monitor (by using the DOS MODE command, for example) while you are in a DOS shell (File | DOS Shell).

- User programs that directly access ports on the inactive monitor's video card aren't supported and can cause unpredictable results.

- When you run or debug programs that explicitly make use of dual monitors, don't use the IDE dual-monitor option (/**D**).

The /E option

TURBO only

Use the /**E** option to change the size of the editor heap. The default size is 28K, the minimum setting; the maximum is 128K. Making the editor heap larger than 28K improves IDE performance only if you're using a slow disk as a swap device. If you have EMS or have placed your swap file on a RAM disk (see /**S** option), don't change the default setting.

The /F option

BP only

With the /**F** option, you can specify a swap file for Borland Pascal's run-time manager (RTM.EXE). For example, if you're compiling an application that requires 4MB of memory, but your computer only has 2MB available, you can specify a virtual-memory 4MB swap file; your application will now have the memory it needs to compile. Legal sizes for the swap file are 1024K to 16384K. This example specifies a 2MB swap file:

    BP /F2048

When you no longer want a virtual-memory swap file, disable this option by specifying a file size of 0:

```
BP /F0
```

The /G option Use the **/G** option to enable a full graphics memory save while you're debugging graphics programs on EGA, VGA, and MCGA systems. With Graphics Screen Save on, the IDE reserves another 8K for the buffer, which is placed in EMS if it's available.

The /L option Use the **/L** option if you're running the IDE on an LCD or plasma screen.

The /N option Use the **/N** option to enable or disable CGA snow checking; the default setting is on. Disable this option if you're using a CGA that doesn't experience snow during screen updates. This option has no effect unless you're using a CGA.

The /O option

TURBO only

Use the **/O** option to change the IDE's overlay heap size. The default is 90K. The minimum size you can adjust this to is 64K; the maximum is 256K. If you have EMS, you can decrease the size of the overlay heap without degrading IDE performance and free more memory for compiling and debugging your programs.

The /P option Use the **/P** option, which controls palette swapping on EGA video adapters, when your program modifies the EGA palette registers. The EGA palette will be restored each time the screen is swapped.

In general, you don't need to use this option unless your program modifies the EGA palette registers or uses BGI to change the palette.

The /R option If the **/R** option is on and the IDE starts up, the last directory you were in the last time you exited the IDE becomes the current directory. The default setting is on. For this option to take effect, you must also choose Options | Environment | Preferences and check the Desktop Auto Save option. If you don't want the IDE to remember your last directory, turn the **/R** option off.

The /S option

If your system has no expanded memory available, use the /**S** option to specify the drive and path of a "fast" swap area, such as a RAM disk (for example, /Sd:\, where *d* is the drive). If no swap directory is specified, a swap file is created in the current directory.

The /T option

To learn about TPUMOVER, read Chapter 1, "Unit mover," in the Tools and Utilities Guide.

Disable the /**T** option if you don't want the IDE to load the run-time library. For TURBO.EXE, the run-time library is TURBO.TPL. For BP.EXE, the run-time library can be TURBO.TPL (real mode), TPW.TPL (Windows), or TPP.TPL (protected mode) depending on the target platform. If the run-time library isn't loaded, you'll need the *System* unit available before you can compile or debug programs. You can increase the IDE capacity of the real-mode IDE by disabling the /**T** option and extracting SYSTEM.TPU from the run-time library using TPUMOVER. If you use the protected-mode IDE, you can do the same by extracting SYSTEM.TPU, SYSTEM.TPW, or SYSTEM.TPP depending on your target plat-form. To read about choosing a target platform, see page 54.

The /W option

TURBO only

Use the /**W** option if you want to change the window heap size. The default setting is 32K. The minimum setting is 24K; the maximum is 64K. Reduce the window heap size to make more memory available for your programs if you don't need a lot of windows open on your desktop. The default gives the IDE good capacity and ample window space.

The /X option

TURBO only

Disable the /**X** option if you don't want the IDE to use expanded memory (EMS). The default setting is on. When this option is enabled, the IDE improves performance by placing overlaid code, editor data, and other system resources in expanded memory.

The /Y option

BP only

You can choose to have the compiler "remember" symbol information between compilations. If this option is on and you make a change to your program, but your next compilation fails, you still have the symbol information available to you from the previous compilation. Therefore, you can still browse through your program to help you determine what the problem is. The default option is on.

Setting startup options in the IDE

You can also set startup options in the IDE itself:

1. Choose Options | Environment | Startup to display the Startup Options dialog box.
2. Select your options and choose OK.

Your startup options will be in effect the next time you start up the IDE.

Exiting the IDE

There are two ways to leave the IDE:

■ To exit the IDE completely, choose File | Exit. If you've made changes that you haven't saved, the IDE prompts you on whether you want to save your programs before exiting.
■ To leave the IDE temporarily to enter commands at the DOS command line, choose File | DOS Shell. The IDE stays in memory but transfers you to DOS. You can enter DOS commands and even run other programs. When you're ready to return to the IDE, type EXIT at the command line and press *Enter*. The IDE reappears just as you left it.

Using the Help system

The Help system gives you easy access to detailed information about the Borland Pascal language, the IDE, the run-time libraries, compiler directives, and so on.

If you've never used Borland language DOS Help systems before, you'll want to bring up a Help screen as you read the next sections. Choose Help | Contents and the Borland Pascal Help Contents screen appears.

Moving around in the Help system

As you look at Help screens you're likely to notice text that appears in a different color than the surrounding text. These are *links*. You can use links to display a new Help screen that presents new information on the linked topic. Choose one of these methods:

- Double-click the link.
- If the Help screen doesn't have buttons:

  Press *Tab* repeatedly until the link is highlighted, then press *Enter*.
- If the Help screen is actually a dialog box with buttons:

  - If you're using a mouse, click the Cross-ref button.

  - If you're using a keyboard, press *Enter*; this chooses the default Cross-ref button. To choose another button, press the *Tab* key until the button you want is selected, then press *Enter*.

A new Help screen appears with information on the topic you selected. You have "jumped" to a new location in the Help system. You might see more links on this screen, which you can select for even more information.

To return to a previous Help screen, choose Help | Previous Topic or press *Alt+F1*.

Asking for Help

You can access Help in several ways:

- Choose Help on the Menu bar or press *Alt+H* to display the Help menu.

  From the Help menu, you can choose to see a Contents screen, an Index screen for the entire Help system, detailed information on the topic your cursor is resting on in the active edit window, or Help on using the Help system. You can also bring up more Help files; see page 42.
- Press *Shift+F1* to display the Borland Pascal Help Index screen.

  The Index screen is very similar to an index in a book. Instead of turning to a page to see information about an indexed topic, however, you choose a topic by double-clicking it or by pressing *Tab* to reach the topic and then pressing *Enter*.
- Press *F1*.

  You get context-sensitive information depending on what you were doing at the time you pressed *F1*—editing, debugging, selecting menu options, and so on.

  If you were in a dialog box, you'll see a Help screen on the option you had selected at the time you pressed *F1*.
- Choose the Help button from within a dialog box.

You get information about the dialog box when you chose the Help button.

- Place your cursor on a term in an edit window and choose Topic Search. Use any of these four methods:

  - Press *Ctrl+F1*.
  - Choose Help | Topic Search.
  - Hold down the *Ctrl* key and click your right mouse button. (You must have customized the *Ctrl*+right mouse button combination first—choose Options | Environment | Mouse and check the Topic Search option.)

To learn about the edit window local menu, see page 49

  - Choose Topic Search on the edit window local menu. (Press *Alt+F10* to display the local menu or click your right mouse button.)

A Help screen appears displaying information about the term your cursor is on in the active edit window.

Copying code examples

The Help system has code examples for each procedure and function. You can copy these examples from the Help system into an edit window. Follow these steps:

1. Display the Help screen for a procedure or function you are interested in.
2. Scroll the Help window until you see the code example in the window.
3. Press *Alt+F10* or click your right mouse button to display the Help local menu.
4. Copy the example:

   - To copy the entire sample code, choose Copy Example.
   - To copy only a portion of the sample code, highlight the code you want to copy and choose Copy.

5. Return to the edit window and choose Edit | Paste, press *Shift+Ins*, or choose Paste on the edit window local menu.

Loading other Help files

The IDE lets you merge other Help files into the Help system. For example, if you want help with Turbo Vision, you can load the Turbo Vision Help file. The IDE merges the indexes for the two

Help files so you can access both the usual Help system and Turbo Vision Help from the Index screen.

To load a new Help system, follow these steps:

1. Choose Help | Files.

    The Install Help Files dialog box appears.

2. Choose New.

    The Help Files dialog box appears. All the Help files in your BIN directory with a .TPH extension appear in the list box. If don't see any Help files, change to the BP\BIN directory.

Repeat this step if you want to select a second Help file also.

3. Double-click the Help file you want to merge into the Help system or select it and press *Enter*.

    The Install Help Files dialog box reappears with the Help file you chose listed in the list box.

4. Choose OK.

5. Choose Help | Index or press *Shift+F1*.

    You might see a brief message on the status line indicating the indexes are merging. When the merging is complete, you can scroll through the Index screen and see that all the topics in the selected Help files are available to you.

To learn about saving your environment, see page 78.

    The indexes remain merged throughout your current session. If you have checked the Environment Auto Save option in the Preferences dialog box (Options | Environment | Preferences), the indexes will remain merged for your next sessions, also. If you don't save your environment, the next time you start up the IDE, the Help index reverts to its original state. In other words, the indexes won't remain merged across sessions.

If no longer want to see a particular Help file's index entries on the Index screen, you can "delete" the Help file:

1. Choose Help | Files.

2. Select the Help file name you no longer want to see.

3. Choose Delete.

4. Choose OK.

Exiting Help

To close a Help window and return to your application, you can choose one of these methods:

- Press *Esc*.
- Click the Help window's Close box.
- Click outside the Help window.

If you want to redisplay your previous Help screen, press *Alt+F1*.

Writing and editing your code

You can open as many windows in the IDE as the amount of memory in your system allows.

Type in text as you would with any editor. To end a line, press *Enter*. When you've entered enough lines to fill the screen, the top line scrolls off the screen.

For a complete list of editing commands, see Appendix A, "Editor reference," in the *Programmer's Reference*.

Configuring the editor

You have several options to modify the behavior of the Borland Pascal editor. Choose Options | Environment | Editor to display the Editor dialog box.

For information about syntax highlighting in the editor, see page 49.

To find out more about each option, select the option and press *F1*. The Help system explains what the option does.

Changing your mind: Undo

The editor has an Undo command that makes it easy to change your mind or correct a mistake. To reverse your previous editing operation, choose Edit | Undo or press *Alt+Backspace*. If you continue to choose Undo, the editor continues to reverse actions. You can even "undo" an Undo command each time you use the Edit | Redo command.

Undo inserts any characters you deleted, deletes any characters you inserted, replaces any characters you overwrote, and moves your cursor back to a prior position. If you undo a block operation, your file appears as it did before you executed the block operation.

Undo doesn't change an option setting that affects more than one window. For example, if you use the *Ins* key to change from Insert to Overwrite mode, then choose Undo, the editor won't change back to Insert mode. But if you delete a character, switch to

Overwrite mode, then select Undo, your previously deleted character reappears.

Grouping undos

The Group Undo option in the Options | Environment | Editor dialog box affects how Undo and its related command, Redo, behave. If you select the Group Undo option, the editor reverses your last *group* of commands when you press *Alt+Backspace* or choose Edit | Undo.

A group is a series of commands of the same type.

Here is an example of how the group option works. If you type MISTAKE and Group Undo is on, Undo deletes the entire word. If Group Undo isn't selected and you type MISTAKE, Undo deletes only the last character, the letter E. You need to press Undo seven times to undo the word MISTAKE when Group Undo is off.

Insertions, deletions, overstrikes, and cursor movements are all groups. Once you change the type of command, the old group ends and a new one begins. To the editor, inserting a carriage return by pressing *Enter* is an insertion followed by a cursor movement. Because the type of editing changed (you inserted characters, then you moved your cursor), the grouping of inserted characters halts when you press *Enter*.

Redoing what you have undone

The Edit | Redo command reverses the effect of the most recent Undo command. Redo is effective immediately only after an Undo or another Redo. A series of Redo commands reverses the effects of a series of Undo commands. Just as it does with Undo, the Group Undo option also affects Redo.

Working with blocks of text

A block of text is any amount of text, from a single character to hundreds of lines, that is selected on your screen. There can be only one block in a window at a time.

Selecting a block

There are at least three ways to select a block of text:

- Drag your mouse over the text you want to select.
- Place your cursor at the beginning of the block, hold down *Shift*, and move your cursor to the end of the block with the arrow keys.
- Click at the beginning of the block, move your cursor to the end of the block using the arrow keys, then hold down *Shift* while you click your mouse again.

If you've used Borland editors in the past, you can also use the old block commands you're used to. See Appendix A, "Editor reference," in the *Programmer's Reference* for a table of Borland-style block commands.

Cutting, copying, and pasting blocks

Once selected, the block can be copied, moved, deleted, or written to a file.

- To cut selected text, press *Shift+Del* or choose Edit | Cut. The selected block is deleted from your text and placed in the Clipboard, a temporary storage location.
- To copy selected text, press *Ctrl+Ins* or choose Edit | Copy. The selected block remains in your text and a copy is placed in the Clipboard ready to paste into your active edit window.
- To paste (copy) text held in the Clipboard into the active edit window, press *Shift+Ins* or choose Edit | Paste. The block held in the Clipboard is pasted at the current cursor position.
- To clear (delete) selected text, press *Ctrl+Del* or choose Edit | Clear. The selected block is deleted from your text and a copy is not placed in the Clipboard. The only way you can recover text that has been cleared is to choose Edit | Undo.

Modifying the behavior of selected blocks

Two options affect the behavior of selected blocks in the editor: Persistent Blocks and Overwrite Blocks. Find them in the Options | Environment | Editor dialog box.

- If Persistent Blocks is on, selected blocks remain selected until you delete or deselect them (or until you select another block).
- If Persistent Blocks is off and you move the cursor after a block is selected, the entire block of text is deselected.
- If Persistent Blocks is on, the Overwrite Blocks setting is ignored.
- If Overwrite Blocks is on and you type a letter, the selected text is replaced with the letter you typed.
- If Overwrite Blocks is off, and you type a letter, the letter is inserted after the selected text.
- If Overwrite Blocks is on *and* Persistent Blocks is off, and you press the *Del* key or the *Backspace* key the entire selected text is cleared.

If you insert text (by pressing a character or pasting from the Clipboard) the entire selected text is replaced with the inserted text.

Searching

You can use the editor to find a text string in your code. To search for a string of text in the active edit window, follow these steps:

1. Choose Search | Find. This opens the Find Text dialog box.
2. Type the string you are looking for into the Text to Find input box.
3. You can also set various search options:

See Help if you need more information about these options.

   ■ The Options check boxes determine if the search
     • Is case sensitive.
     • Looks for whole words only.
     • Uses regular expressions. See Appendix A in the *Programmer's Reference* for information about using regular expressions in search strings.
   ■ The Scope radio buttons control how much of the file you search—the whole file or only the selected text.
   ■ The Direction radio buttons control whether you do a forward or backward search.
   ■ The Origin radio buttons control where the search begins.

4. Choose OK to perform the search.
5. If you want to search for the same item again, choose Search | Search Again.

By default, the word your cursor rests on in your source code appears in the Text to Find input box when you display the Find dialog box. If you don't want this to happen, do this:

1. Choose Options | Environment | Editor.
2. Uncheck the Find Text at Cursor option.
3. Choose OK.

When you display the Find dialog box, the word your cursor rests on appears in the input box. If you want to search for a phrase or group of words instead of a single word, while your cursor is in the Find Text input box, press the → key. More text appears in the input box as if the text were being "pulled" from the edit window.

Search and replace

To search for a string of text and replace it with another string, choose Search | Replace. Select options in the dialog box as you did for Search, but also include a replacement string in the New Text box.

If you want to replace all occurrences of a string in your file, choose Change All. If you check the Prompt on Replace option, the editor searches until it finds the string you indicated and asks if you want to replace it. To stop the operation, choose Cancel when the search pauses.

If you don't check the Prompt on Replace option, all the search strings are replaced with the new text. It's a good idea to select the Whole Words Only option if you don't use the Prompt on Replace option. That way you won't risk replacing characters in a middle of a word—something you probably don't want to happen.

Delimiter pair matching

Sometimes you don't need to search for text, but for the match to a particular delimiter (a brace, parenthesis, bracket, single quotation mark, double quotation mark, or the parenthesis-asterisk combination that denotes a comment). Suppose you have a complicated expression with a number of nested expressions and you want to make sure all the parentheses are properly balanced. Here's what to do:

1. Place the cursor on the delimiter.
2. Press *Ctrl+Q[*.

The editor immediately moves the cursor to the delimiter that matches the one you selected. If it moves to a delimiter other than the one you expected, you know you have made a mistake.

If there is no mate for the delimiter you've selected, the editor doesn't move the cursor.

There are actually two match-pair editing commands: one for forward matching (*Ctrl+Q[*) and the other for backward matching (*Ctrl+Q]*).

If you place your cursor on a single or double quote, the editor doesn't know if it should search forward or backward to find its mate. You must specify the correct match-pair command for single and double quotes.

It doesn't matter which match-pair command you use to search for braces, brackets, and parentheses. The editor knows which way to search for the mate.

Here is an illustrated example of pair matching:

Figure 4.1
Search for match to square
bracket or parenthesis

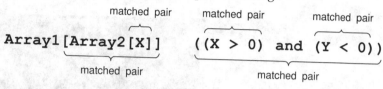

Going to a line number

The editor keeps track of what line your cursor is on and displays the line number on the edit window status line. A quick way to jump to a place in your file is to use the Go to Line Number command:

1. Choose Search | Go to Line Number.
2. Type in the number of the line where you want to go.
3. Choose OK.

Using the edit window local menu

Many of the tasks you perform while you're working in an edit window are conveniently located on the edit window *local menu*. While an edit window is active, you can display the local menu two ways:

■ Press *Alt+F10*.
■ Click your right mouse button.

The IDE has other local menus as well. As you read about using Help, browsing, and debugging, you'll learn where other local menus are available.

Syntax highlighting

As you write or edit your Pascal program, some of the code appears in different colors on your screen. For example, Borland Pascal reserved words appear in white while the remainder of the text appears in yellow. This color coding makes it easier to quickly identify parts of your code.

Coloring your text To change the color of an element, follow these steps:

1. Choose Options | Environment | Colors and the Colors dialog box appears.

Figure 4.2
Colors dialog box

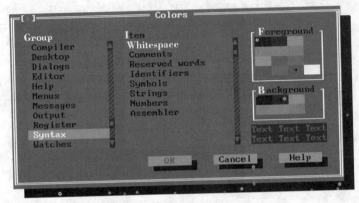

The list box on the left displays all the groups of items you can color in the IDE.

2. Scroll the Group list box entries until you see the Syntax group. Select the Syntax group, and the Pascal code elements you can color appear in the Item list box.

3. Select the item you want to change in the Item list box.

4. Select the foreground and background color you want for that item.

   ■ To select a foreground color with your mouse, click the color you want in the Foreground color matrix. To select the color with your keyboard, press *Tab* until the Foreground color matrix is selected, then use the arrow keys to select a color.

   ■ To select a background color, choose the color you want in the Background color matrix.

As soon as you make a color selection, you'll see it reflected in the sample text window.

5. Choose OK.

Selecting files to highlight

By default, only files with a .PAS or .INC extension display syntax highlighting. You might want to highlight other file types.

To change the type of files displayed with syntax highlighting:

1. Choose Options | Environment | Editor.
2. Change the text in the Highlight Extensions box.

   Any DOS file name, including one with wildcards, is valid. You can specify multiple file names; place a semicolon between each one.

Disabling syntax highlighting

If you don't want to use syntax highlighting, you can turn it off:

1. Choose Options | Environment | Editor.
2. Uncheck the Syntax Highlight option.

 Normal text color is changed by altering the colors for the Editor | Normal Text option in the Options | Environment | Colors dialog box. If you don't turn off syntax highlighting, changing the normal text color has no effect.

Printing your code

When you want a printed copy of your code, choose File | Print. The IDE expands tabs (replaces tab characters with the appropriate number of spaces) and then prints your file.

Syntax highlighting printing

It's possible to print your text so that syntax elements are highlighted. Your output must go through the PRNFLTR.EXE filter program before it prints:

1. Choose File | Printer Setup.
2. If PRNFLTR.EXE isn't on your path or in your current directory, add the current path information to the PRNFLTR entry in the Filter Path input box.
3. In the Command Line input box, you can indicate either an Epson, HP LaserJet, or PostScript printer.

   ■ If you have an Epson printer, enter this:

   ```
   $NOSWAP /EPSON
   ```

- If you have an HP LaserJet, enter this:

  `$NOSWAP /HP`
- If you have a PostScript printer, enter this:

  `$NOSWAP /PS`

  If you have a different type of printer, you can modify PRNFLTR.PAS to accept the codes your printer sends it.
4. Check the Send Highlighting Escape Codes option.
5. Choose OK.
6. Choose File | Print.

   If Syntax Highlight is on, your text prints with syntax elements highlighted.

Working with files

As you program in the IDE, you create new files, open existing ones, and save them. Table 2.1 summarizes the basic file-management tasks:

Table 4.1
File operations

Operation	Description
File	New	Opens a new edit window and gives it a temporary name
File	Open	Opens an existing file or creates a new one with a name you specify
File	Save	Saves the file in the active edit window to disk
File	Save As	Saves the file in the active edit window under a different name
File	Save All	Saves all modified files

Opening files

To open a file, follow these steps:

1. Choose File | Open and the Open a File dialog box appears. You can then take any of the following actions to specify a file to open:
   - Type a full file name in the input box.

- Type a file name with wildcards. This filters the Files list to match your file specification. In the Files list, select the file name you want to edit.

- Press ↓ to display a history list of file specifications or file names you entered earlier. Select the file name or specification you want. Selecting a file specification displays files that match that specification.

- View the contents of other directories by double-clicking a directory name in the file list. Select the name of the file you want to edit.

2. Once the file name you want to edit is selected in the input box, choose Open or Replace. Open loads the file into a new edit window; Replace replaces the contents of the active edit window with the selected file.

You can also just press *Enter* once the file is selected, or simply double-click the name of the file you want when you see it listed, and the file opens.

If you open one or more files and then close them, you'll see them listed at the bottom of the File menu, up to a maximum of five files. If you select one of these file names on the menu, the file opens in an edit window. When you work with many open files, you can close some, yet open them again quickly using the list and reduce clutter on your desktop.

You can choose to have your default directory change to the directory the file you open is in. This mimics they way the Windows environment behaves:

1. Choose Options | Environment | Preferences.
2. Check the Change Dir on Open option.
3. Choose OK.

Opening the file at the cursor

The IDE gives you a quick way to open a file whose name is in your source code. You'll find this handy when you want to look at the code of a unit or Include file your program uses.

1. Place your cursor on the name of the file you want to open.
2. Press *Ctrl+Enter* or display the edit window local menu and choose Open File at Cursor.

Compiling and running

The IDE gives you several ways to create an executable program, unit, or, if you're using the protected-mode IDE, a dynamic-link library. You can

- Compile the current file with (Compile | Compile)
- Compile all changed files (Compile | Make)
- Compile all files in your project (Compile | Build)
- Compile and run your program (Run | Run)

Each of these options is suitable for a particular situation. The following sections will help you decide which option you need.

Choosing a target

If you're using BP.EXE, before you compile your program, you need to tell the IDE what kind of application you are creating: a DOS real-mode, a Windows, or a DOS protected-mode application. The type of application you are creating is your *target platform*, or simply your *target*.

TURBO.EXE can create real-mode applications only.

To select a target:

1. Choose Compile | Target.
2. In the Target dialog box, select the target platform of your choice.
3. Choose OK.

 When you compile a unit, the file-name extension of the resulting object code differs depending on your target:

Table 4.2
Compiled unit file-name extensions

Target	Unit object-code file extension
DOS real mode	.TPU
Windows	.TPW
DOS protected mode	.TPP

Compiling

The Compile | Compile command compiles only the file in the active edit window. While your program compiles, a status box pops up to display the compilation progress and results. When compiling and linking is complete, press any key to put the status box away. If an error occurred, you'll see an error message at the top of the edit window and your cursor will be positioned on the line in your code where the error occurred.

If the file you are compiling depends on a unit that isn't up-to-date, your file won't compile.

Choosing a destination

TURBO only

If you're using the real-mode IDE, you can choose to compile your program to disk or to memory with the Compile | Destination command. If you choose to compile to disk, your executable code is stored on disk as an .EXE file. Compiling to disk increases the memory available in the IDE to compile and debug your program. If you choose to compile to memory, your program is stored in memory, and, if you don't save it, is lost when you exit the IDE.

If you compile to disk, the resulting .EXE or .TPU files are stored in the same directory as the source files, or in the EXE and TPU directory (Options | Directories), if one is specified.

Making

If your program includes more than just the code in the active window—for example, it includes a primary file, one or more units, external assembly language modules, and so on—you might want to *make* your program. Make compiles all code that has been modified since it was last compiled.

Read about creating DLLs in Chapter 11, "Dynamic-link libraries," in the Language Guide.

The Compile | Make command creates an .EXE file or unit. If you're using the protected-mode IDE and Windows is your target, it can also create a dynamic-link library (DLL). These are the rules Make uses:

See more about primary files on page 81.

■ If a primary file has been specified, it is compiled; otherwise, the file in the active edit window is compiled. The IDE checks all files upon which the file being compiled depends to make sure they exist and are current.

Find out more about units in Chapter 7, "Borland Pascal units."

■ If the source file for a given unit has been modified since the .TPU, .TPW, or .TPP (object code) file was created, that unit is recompiled.

■ If the interface for a given unit has been changed, all other units that depend on it are recompiled.

■ If a unit links in an .OBJ file (external routines), and the .OBJ file is newer than the unit's .TPU, .TPW, or .TPP file, the unit is recompiled.

■ If a unit contains an Include file and the Include file is newer than that unit's .TPU, .TPW, or .TPP file, the unit is recompiled.

If the compiler can't locate the source code for a unit, the unit isn't compiled and is used as is.

If you've chosen to compile to memory with the DOS real-mode IDE, any units recompiled with Make have their .TPU files updated on disk.

Building

The Compile | Build command rebuilds all the components of your program, whether or not they're current.

This command is similar to Compile | Make except it compiles everything, even if a file doesn't change. If you stop a Build command by pressing *Ctrl+Break* or get errors that halt the build, you can pick up where it left off by choosing Compile | Make.

If you've chosen to compile to memory with the DOS real-mode IDE, any units recompiled with Build have their .TPU files updated on disk.

Running

After you create an executable file, you'll want to try out your program with the Run | Run command. You really don't have to compile your program first and then run it, however. Run also "makes" your program if your code changed since you last compiled it, and then executes it.

 If your program is a DOS protected-mode application, you must have the files DPMI16BI.OVL and RTM.EXE in your current directory or on your DOS path, or your program won't run. You can distribute these files with your finished application for resale.

Passing parameters to your program

You can pass command-line parameters to your program when you run it. Choose Run | Parameters to display a Parameters dialog box and type in the list of parameters you want your program to use.

Compiler and linker options

The IDE lets you choose from several options that affect the way your code is compiled. Choose Options | Compiler to display the Compiler Options dialog box. If you are unsure what a particular option does, select it in the dialog box and a help hint appears on the status line. Press *F1* to display in-depth information about this option or choose Help for information about the entire Compiler Options dialog box.

Figure 4.3
Compiler Options dialog box

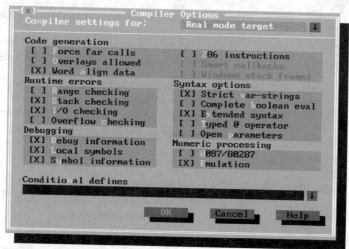

Compiler Options

Compiler settings for: Real mode target

Code generation
[ ] Force far calls   [ ] 286 instructions
[ ] Overlays allowed   [ ] Smart callbacks
[X] Word align data   [ ] Windows stack frames
Runtime errors   Syntax options
[ ] Range checking   [X] Strict var-strings
[X] Stack checking   [ ] Complete boolean eval
[X] I/O checking   [X] Extended syntax
[ ] Overflow checking   [ ] Typed @ operator
Debugging   [ ] Open parameters
[X] Debug information   Numeric processing
[X] Local symbols   [ ] 8087/80287
[X] Symbol information   [X] Emulation

Conditional defines

OK   Cancel   Help

Specifying compiler options for a target platform

Which compiler options you choose depends heavily on what your target platform is. For example, if you're creating a DOS real-mode application, you might want to enable the use of overlays, something you don't need for a Windows or DOS protected-mode program.

The TURBO.EXE Compiler Options menu won't have the Compiler Settings For option.

You can set standard compiler options for your preferred target platform:

1. Click the ↓ of the Compiler Settings For drop-down list box, or press the ↓ cursor key when the Compiler Settings For list box is selected.

2. Choose the target platform of your choice.

The IDE automatically checks commonly used options. You can override the IDE's selections at any time.

If a compiler option is incompatible with the selected target platform, the option is dimmed and you can't select it.

Setting compiler options for all targets

If you want a particular compiler option to be set regardless of which target platform you choose, do this:

1. Select All Targets as the Compiler Settings For option.
2. Check or uncheck the compiler option you want set.

For example, if you want to use 286 instructions for all platforms, choose All and then check the 286 instructions option.

When you select All Targets, you might see a question mark (?) appear in some of the check boxes. This tells you that an option setting isn't the same for all three platforms. You can then change that option to make it the same for all platforms, or you can leave it as it is.

Specifying linker options

How your code is linked depends on the settings in the Linker Options dialog box. Choose Options | Linker to display it. Choose Help if you need more details.

Inserting compiler directives in code

There is a second way to specify how your code is compiled. Instead of using dialog boxes to set options, you can insert a *compiler directive* in your code. For example, you can turn range checking on for your program by choosing the Range Checking option in the Options | Compiler dialog box, or you can put the {$R+} compiler directive in your code. For a complete discussion of compiler directives and how to use them, see Chapter 2, "Compiler directives," in the *Programmer's Reference*.

Compiler directives that you insert in your code take precedence over compiler options you set in the IDE. For example, if you have Range Checking turned on in the IDE, but your program includes the {R-} directive, your program compiles with range checking disabled.

Optimizing code

A number of compiler options influence both the size and the speed of your code because they insert error-checking and error-handling code into your program. Although these type of options are good to use while you're developing your program, you might gain speed and smaller code size without them.

Here are those options with their settings for code optimization. The corresponding compiler directive follows each mention of a compiler option. Consider using these options for your final compilation:

- Word Align Data ({$A+}) aligns variables and type constants on word boundaries, resulting in faster memory access on 80x86 systems.

- Turning off Complete Boolean Evaluation ({$B-}) produces code that can run faster, depending upon how you set up your Boolean expressions.

- When Emulation is off ({$E-}), the compiler won't link with a run-time library that emulates an 80x87. It must either use the 80x87 if it is present, or use only the standard 6-byte type *Real*. Emulation isn't used when compiling Windows applications; if the Emulation directive is present, the compiler ignores it.

- When 80286 Code Generation is on ({$G+}), the compiler uses additional instructions of the 80286 to improve code generation. Programs compiled this way can't run on 8088 and 8086 processors.

- When I/O Checking is off ({$I-}), the compiler doesn't check for errors. By calling the predefined function *IOResult*, you can handle I/O errors yourself.

- When Numeric Processing is off ({$N-}), the compiler generates code capable of performing all floating-point operations using the built-in, 6-byte type *Real*. When the Numeric Processing is on ({$N+}), the compiler uses the 80x87 coprocessor or emulates the coprocessor in software routines instead, depending on whether an 80x87 is present. The resulting code can use the four additional real types (*Single*, *Double*, *Extended*, and *Comp*).

- When Range Checking is off ({$R-}), the compiler doesn't check for array-subscripting errors and the assignment of out-of-range values.

- When Stack Checking is off ({$S-}), the compiler doesn't ensure there is enough space on the stack for each procedure or function call.

- When Relaxed String Var Checking is on ({$V-}), the compiler doesn't check **var** parameters that are strings. This lets you pass actual parameter strings that are of a different length than the type defined for the formal **var** parameter.

■ When Extended Syntax is on (({**$X+**})), you can use function calls as statements because the result of a function call can be discarded.

Optimizing your code using these options has two advantages. First, it makes your code smaller and faster. Second, it lets you do some things you usually can't do. These options all have risks, however, so use them carefully and turn them back on if your program behaves strangely.

Conditional compilation

To make your job easier, Borland Pascal offers conditional compilation. This means you can decide which portions of your program to compile based on options or defined symbols.

For a complete reference to conditional directives, refer to Chapter 2, "Compiler directives," in the Programmer's Reference.

The conditional directives are similar in format to the compiler directives you're accustomed to. They take the following format,

```
{$directive arg}
```

where *directive* is the directive (such as **DEFINE**, **IFDEF**, and so on), and *arg* is the argument, if any. There *must* be a separator (blank, tab) between *directive* and *arg*. Table 4.3 lists all the conditional directives, with their meanings.

Table 4.3
Conditional compilation
directives

Directive	Description
{**$DEFINE** *symbol*}	Defines *symbol* for other directives
{**$UNDEF** *symbol*}	Removes definition of *symbol*
{**$IFDEF** *symbol*}	Compiles following code if *symbol* is defined
{**$IFNDEF** *symbol*}	Compiles following code if *symbol* isn't defined
{**$IFOPT** x+}	Compiles following code if directive *x* is enabled
{**$IFOPT** x-}	Compiles following code if directive *x* is disabled
{**$ELSE**}	Compiles following code if previous **IF**xxx isn't *True*
{**$ENDIF**}	Marks end of **IF**xxx or **ELSE** section

The DEFINE and UNDEF
directives

The **IFDEF** and **IFNDEF** directives test whether a given symbol is defined. You define these symbols using the **DEFINE** and **UNDEF** directives. (You can also define symbols on the command line and in the IDE.)

To define a symbol, insert the following directive in your program:

```
{$DEFINE symbol}
```

symbol follows the usual rules for identifiers as far as length, characters allowed, and other specifications. For example, you might write

```
{$DEFINE debug}
```

This defines the symbol *debug* for the remainder of the module being compiled, or until the following statement is encountered:

```
{$UNDEF debug}
```

As you might guess, **UNDEF** "undefines" a symbol. If the symbol isn't defined, **UNDEF** has no effect.

Defining conditional symbols in the IDE

Rather than inserting a **DEFINE** directive in your code, you can also define conditional symbols in the Conditional Defines input box (Options | Compiler). Define multiple symbols by entering them in the input box, separated by semicolons. For example, the next example defines two conditional symbols, *TestCode* and *DebugCode*.

```
TestCode;DebugCode
```

Predefined symbols

In addition to any symbols you define, you also can test certain symbols the compiler has defined. Table 4.4 lists these symbols.

Table 4.4
Predefined conditional
symbols

Symbol	Indicates
CPU86	This version of Borland Pascal is for the 80x86 family of processors.
CPU87	An 80x87 numeric coprocessor is present.
DPMI	This version is for the DOS protected-mode environment. This symbol is available to BP.EXE when creating DOS protected-mode applications.
MSDOS	This version is for the MS-DOS operating system. This symbol is available only to BP.EXE when creating DOS real or protected-mode applications and to TURBO.EXE.
VER70	This is version 7.0 of the compiler.
WINDOWS	This version is for the Windows operating environment. This symbol is available to BPW.EXE and BP.EXE when Windows is the target.

See Chapter 2, "Compiler directives," in the *Programmer's Reference* for more information about the compiler's predefined conditional symbols.

The IFxxx, ELSE, and ENDIF symbols

The idea behind conditional directives is that you want to select some amount of source code to be compiled if a particular symbol is (or isn't) defined or if a particular option is (or isn't) enabled. The general format is as follows where **IFxxx** is **IFDEF**, **IFNDEF**, or **IFOPT**, followed by the appropriate argument, and *source code* is any amount of Pascal source code:

```
{$IFxxx}
   source code
{$ENDIF}
```

If the expression in the **IFxxx** directive is *True*, then *source code* is compiled; otherwise, it is ignored as if it had been commented out of your program.

Often you have alternate chunks of source code. If the expression is *True*, you want one chunk compiled, and if it's *False*, you want the other one compiled. The compiler lets you do this with the **$ELSE** directive:

```
{$IFxxx}
   source code A
{$ELSE}
   source code B
{$ENDIF}
```

If the expression in **IFxxx** is True, *source code A* is compiled; otherwise *source code B* is compiled.

All **IFxxx** directives must be completed within the same source file, which means they can't start in one source file and end in another. However, an **IFxxx** *directive can encompass an Include file*:

```
{$IFxxx}
{$I file1.pas}
{$ELSE}
{$I file2.pas}
{$ENDIF}
```

That way, you can select alternate Include files based on some condition.

You can nest **IFxxx..ENDIF** constructs so that you can have something like this:

```
{$IFxxx}                                        { First IF directive }
  ⋮
{$IFxxx}                                        { Second IF directive }
  ⋮
{$ENDIF}                                  { Terminates second IF directive }
  ⋮
{$ENDIF}                                  { Terminates first IF directive }
```

The IFDEF and IFNDEF directives

The **IFDEF** and **IFNDEF** directives let you conditionally compile code based on whether those symbols are defined or undefined.

It is common to use the **IFDEF** and **IFNDEF** directives to insert debugging information into your compiled code. For example, if you put the following code at the start of each unit:

```
{$IFDEF debug}
{$D+,L+}
{$ELSE}
{$D-,L-}
{$ENDIF}
```

and the following directive at the start of your program:

```
{$DEFINE debug}
```

and compile your program, complete debugging information is generated by the compiler for use with Turbo Debugger. In a similar fashion, you can have sections of code that you want compiled only if you are debugging; in that case, you would write

```
{$IFDEF debug}
  source code
{$ENDIF}
```

source code is compiled only if *debug* is defined at that point.

The IFOPT directive

You might want to include or exclude code, depending on which compiler options (range checking, I/O checking, and so on) have been selected. You do that with the **IFOPT** directive, which takes two forms:

```
{$IFOPT x+}
```

and

```
{$IFOPT x-}
```

See Chapter 2 in the Programmer's Reference, "Compiler directives," for a complete description of all compiler options.

where *x* is one of the compiler options. With the first form, the following code is compiled if the compiler option is currently enabled; with the second, the code is compiled if the option is currently disabled. So, for example, you could use the following code to select data type for the listed variables, based on whether or not 80x87 support is enabled:

```
var
  {$IFOPT N+}
    Radius,Circ,Area: Double;
  {$ELSE}
    Radius,Circ,Area: Real;
  {$ENDIF}
```

Browsing through your code

BP only The DOS protected-mode IDE has a new programming tool, the ObjectBrowser. It lets you explore the objects and units in your programs and much more. Even if the applications you develop don't use object-oriented programming, you'll still find the ObjectBrowser an extremely valuable tool. You can browse through your object hierarchies, units, and all the procedures, functions, variables, types, constants, and other symbols your program uses. Using the ObjectBrowser, you can do these things:

- You can view the object hierarchies in your application, then select an object and view all the procedures, functions, and other symbols it contains. As you examine a symbol, you can choose to list all references to it in your program and, if you want, go directly to where it is used in your source code.

- You can list the global symbols your program uses and see their declarations. If you select one, you can list all references to it in your program and, if you want, go directly to where it is used in your source code.

- You can list all the units your program uses, then select one and list all the symbols in its interface part.

- You can select a symbol in your source code, then view its details by holding down the *Ctrl* key and clicking the right mouse button.

- You can open multiple browser windows, compare the symbols displayed in different windows, and then return to a previously opened browser window.

Before you use the ObjectBrowser, be sure to check these options in the Options | Compiler dialog box:

- Debug Information
- Local Symbols
- Symbol Information

Also make sure the Integrated Debugging/Browsing option is checked in the Debugging/Browsing dialog box (Options | Debugger).

Compile the program you want to browse.

To activate the ObjectBrowser, choose Objects, Unit, or Globals on the Search menu. You can also place your cursor on a symbol in your code and choose Search | Symbol to bring up the ObjectBrowser.

You can choose to have the compiler "remember" symbol information between compilations. If this option is on and you make a change to your program, but your next compilation fails, you still have the symbol information available to you from the previous compilation. Therefore, you can still browse through your program to help you determine what the problem is. To have the compiler keep symbol information between compilations:

Because Preserve Symbols is a startup option, a change to this setting won't take effect until you exit the IDE and then start it again.

1. Choose Options | Environment | Startup.
2. Check the Preserve Symbols option; this is the default setting.
3. Choose OK.
4. Choose File | Exit to exit the IDE.
5. Start the IDE again.

You can also choose Browse Symbol at Cursor from the edit window local menu to quickly browse the symbol your cursor is resting on in your code.

If you have a mouse, you'll find browsing through your code more convenient if you set up your right mouse button to activate the ObjectBrowser. Then you can hold down the *Ctrl* key while you use your right mouse button to click an object, procedure, function, variable, or other symbol in your source code and inspect it (view its details).

To set up your mouse for browsing, follow these steps:

1. Choose Options | Environment | Mouse.

2. Select Browse as the Ctrl + Right Mouse Button option.

3. Choose OK.

Browsing objects

For detailed information about using object types, refer to Chapter 9, "Object-oriented programming."

Search | Objects opens a window that displays all of the objects used in your program, arranged in a hierarchical structure. At the top of the window, the ObjectBrowser shows the base type and displays descendants beneath and to the right of the base type. The connecting lines help to clarify ancestor and descendant relationships.

Figure 4.4
Viewing the object hierarchy
of an application

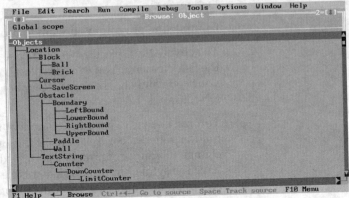

```
 File  Edit  Search  Run  Compile  Debug  Tools  Options  Window  Help
[ ]                              Browse: Object                        2 [ ]
Global scope
 | |
 Objects
  └─Location
     ├─Block
     │  ├─Ball
     │  └─Brick
     ├─Cursor
     │  └─SaveScreen
     ├─Obstacle
     │  ├─Boundary
     │  │  ├─LeftBound
     │  │  ├─LowerBound
     │  │  ├─RightBound
     │  │  └─UpperBound
     │  ├─Paddle
     │  └─Wall
     └─TextString
        └─Counter
           ├─DownCounter
           └─LimitCounter
 F1 Help  ◄┘ Browse  Ctrl+◄┘ Go to source  Space Track source  F10 Menu
```

If your object hierarchy is large, you can choose to not display the descendants of a particular object.

■ Using the keyboard, do this:

1. Select the object.
2. Press the – (minus) key.

■ With a mouse, simply click the horizontal line that attaches the object to the hierarchy.

Now the object displays a + (plus sign) next to it and is highlighted, indicating that descendants of this object are not displayed.

You can display the descendants of the object again.

■ Using the keyboard:

1. Select an object that is prefaced with a + sign.
2. Press the + key.

■ With a mouse, click the horizontal line that attaches the object to the hierarchy.

The descendants of the object reappear.

From the object hierarchy, you can view all the symbols declared in a single object. Select the object and press *Enter* or double-click the object.

As you view the symbols declared in an object, you can choose to see different views:

■ Click the letter I at the top of the ObjectBrowser window or press *Ctrl+I* to display inheritance information for the object you're browsing.
■ Click the letter R at the top of the window or press *Ctrl+R* to display a list of the program or unit lines where the symbol is referenced.
■ Click the letter S or press *Ctrl+S* to display the scope of the object.

To find a symbol in a list of displayed symbols, type the first letters of the symbol's name; your cursor then moves to the symbol quickly.

You might find that you need to change the path for the Include and unit directories in the Options | Directories dialog so that the ObjectBrowser can find where your source files are located.

If you modify your source code by adding or deleting program lines after you have opened a browser window, it's best to recompile your program. Although the ObjectBrowser can still track symbol information after you modify the source code, the source code line numbers displayed on the edit window aren't updated unless you recompile your program.

Changing how the ObjectBrowser displays information

You have considerable control as to how the ObjectBrowser displays information.

You can choose which symbols the ObjectBrowser displays:

1. Choose Options | Browser to display the Browser Options dialog box.
2. In the Symbols group, check only the symbols you want to see displayed in the ObjectBrowser. You can also choose to see symbols inherited from an object's ancestors.

3. Choose OK.

Only the symbols you selected can appear in the ObjectBrowser.

You can also select which symbols appear only in the current browser window. Choose Options on the browser window local menu to display the Local Browser Options dialog box or press *Ctrl+O* when a browser window is displayed.

If you select types, variables, and procedures as the type of symbols you want to see, and then browse through the Location object in the program titled BREAKOUT.PAS (a sample demonstration program in the EXAMPLES\DOS\BREAKOUT directory), you see the following symbol information displayed:

Figure 4.5
Viewing symbol information

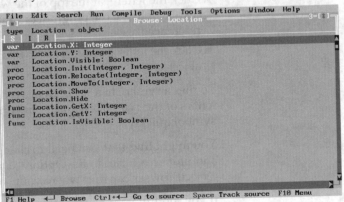

The abbreviations to the left of the listed symbols represent the kind of symbol displayed. Note that turning the procedure symbols off also turns functions off.

Symbol	Meaning
const	Constant
func	Function
label	Label
proc	Procedure
type	Type
var	Variable or a typed constant

To display the previous browser window, choose Search | Previous Browser or press *Ctrl+P*.

When you browse a selected symbol, the ObjectBrowser window displays scope information by default. If you prefer to see reference information as the default setting:

1. Choose Options | Browser.
2. Select Reference as the Preferred Pane option.
3. Choose OK.

By default, the ObjectBrowser displays complete declaration information for the symbol being inspected. You can view all fields and methods of records and objects, including fully qualified identifiers. If you don't want to see the identifiers fully qualified:

You won't see fully qualified identifiers unless you've checked Inherited in the Browser Options dialog box (Options | Browser).

1. Choose Options | Browser.
2. Uncheck the Qualified Symbols display option.
3. Choose OK.

By default, the ObjectBrowser displays identifiers in the Scope pane in the order they are declared. If you prefer that all identifiers appear in alphabetical order, do this:

1. Choose Options | Browser.
2. Check the Sort Always display option.
3. Choose OK.

Identifiers will be sorted by name only, not by their fully qualified names. For example, this list of identifiers is considered to be in alphabetical order:

```
THELPFILE.DONE
TOBJECT.FREE
THELPFILE.INDEX: PHELP
```

When you open a browser window, then browse a symbol listed in it, a new browser window opens, but the previous browser window remains. You can change this behavior so that the new browser window replaces the the current one:

1. Choose Options | Browser.
2. Check the Replace Current sub-browsing option.
3. Choose OK.

To have the current browser window remain when you select a symbol listed in it to browse:

1. Choose Options | Browser.
2. Check the New Browser sub-browsing option.
3. Choose OK.

You might prefer to use either the Replace Current or New Browser options most of the time, but occasionally use the other option. You can choose the alternate option very quickly:

1. Hold down the *Shift* key.
2. Select your next browsing action.

   For example, if the New Browser option is in effect, when you hold down the *Shift* key, the next browser window you open replaces the current one.

Tracking and editing line references

When the ObjectBrowser displays reference information, you can choose to edit the program line displayed in a reference or you can track references to a symbol. Tracking means the IDE highlights one program line after another in your source code as you move through the references in the browser window.

To edit the program line displayed in a reference:

1. Select the reference in the browser window.
2. Press *Ctrl+Enter* or press *Ctrl+G*.

   Your cursor jumps to the program line in the source code referenced in the browser window. You can now edit the program line.

The Close On Go To Source option also affects the Messages window, see page 77.

By default, the ObjectBrowser window closes when your cursor jumps to the program line in the source code. If you prefer that the browser window remains open, uncheck the Close On Go To Source option in the Preferences dialog box.

To track program lines,

1. In the browser window, select the reference you want to track.
2. Press *Spacebar*.

The Auto Track Source option also affects the Messages window, see page 77.

If you always want to track your references in your source code, check Auto Track Source in the Options group of the Preferences dialog box. Then when you scroll through your references, program lines are highlighted in your source code automatically; you don't have to press *Spacebar*.

How program lines referenced in a browser window are tracked depends on how you set tracking options in the Options | Environment | Preferences dialog box: If the referenced file isn't in an edit window, the IDE opens the file and it appears either in a new edit window or in a current edit window.

Source Tracking options also affect the Messages window and the Integrated debugger.

- If you want the file to appear in a new edit window, choose New Window as the Source Tracking option.
- If you want the file to replace the current one in the active edit window, choose Current Window as the Source Tracking option.

 If the selected unit is stored in Borland Pascal's run-time library or is one of the standard units, you won't be able to view or edit the source code because these units have been compiled with the symbol information off.

Browsing units

For detailed information about program units, refer to Chapter 7, "Borland Pascal units."

Search | Units opens a window that displays the units used in your program, listed in alphabetical order. Select a specific unit and press *Enter* or double-click the unit to browse through the symbols declared in the interface section of the unit. Just as you can with objects, you can view scope or reference information for a symbol. As long as the referenced unit isn't one of the standard units that comes with Borland Pascal, and it has been compiled so that it includes all the necessary integrated debugging/browsing information, you can either track or edit the source code where the unit is referenced.

In the the following figure, the unit *Walls* is declared in line 4 of WALLS.PAS and is called on line 37 of BREAKOUT.PAS.

Figure 4.6
Viewing the units in your
application

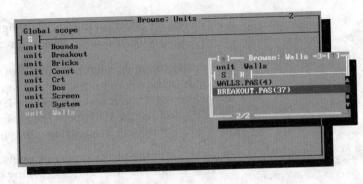

Browsing global symbols

Search | Globals opens a window that displays the global symbols used in your program, listed in alphabetical order. Just as you can with objects, you can open additional ObjectBrowser windows to view program line references to that symbol, the symbol's declarations, and, for objects, the inheritance hierarchy. When reference information is displayed, you can track or edit program lines.

For example, this figure shows a list of the global symbols used in the program BREAKOUT.PAS:

Figure 4.7
Viewing global symbols used
in your program

```
┌[ ]══════════════════ Browse: Globals ═══════════════2═[↑]═┐
│ Global scope                                               │
│├ S ┤                                                       ▲
│ func   Abs(...)                                            │
│ func   Addr(...)                                           │
│ const  AnyFile = 63                                        │
│ proc   Append(...)                                         │
│ const  Archive = 32                                        │
│ func   ArcTan(...)                                         │
│ proc   Assign(...)                                         │
│ proc   AssignCrt(var Text)                                 │
│ func   Assigned(...)                                       │
│ var    b: Ball                                             │
│ type   Ball = object(Block)                                │
│ var    Balls: DownCounter                                  │
│ proc   Beep                                                │
│ const  Black = 0                                           │
│ const  Blink = 128                                         │
│ type   Block = object(Location)                            │
│ proc   BlockRead(...)                                      │
│ proc   BlockWrite(...)                                     │
│ const  Blue = 1                                            ▼
└────────────────────────────────────────────────────────────┘
```

Browsing a symbol in your source code

You can browse a symbol in your source code. Place your cursor on the symbol and choose one of these methods:

- Choose Symbol from the Search menu to display the Browse Symbol dialog box. Accept the symbol listed in the dialog box, or enter another symbol and choose OK.
- Press *Alt+F10* or click your right mouse button to display the edit window local menu, and choose Browse Symbol at Cursor.
- If you've set up your right mouse button to browse symbols (choose Options | Environment | Mouse and select Browse Symbols), hold down the *Ctrl* key and click the right mouse button.

The type of information you see displayed depends on the type of information available for the symbol you selected:

- If the symbol you selected has no scope information available, the ObjectBrowser displays reference information for the symbol. For example, only reference information is available for a simple constant.
- If the symbol you selected does have scope information available, the ObjectBrowser displays scope information for the symbol. It also gives you the option to see reference information.
- If the symbol you selected is a structured type, the Object-Browser displays scope information for the type. It also gives you the options to see inheritance and reference information. If you select to see the inheritance information, you'll see the immediate ancestor of the type and immediate descendants, if any.

If you have selected a structured type to browse, the Object-Browser displays fully qualified names if these two conditions are met:

- The Inherited symbol option is checked in the Browser Options dialog box (Options | Browser) or in the Local Browser Options dialog box (browser window local menu | Options).
- The Qualified Symbols option is checked in the Browser Options dialog box (Options | Browser) or in the Local Browser Options dialog box (browser window local menu | Options).

For example, this figure displays the full declaration scope information for the variable *b* of type *Ball*:

Figure 4.8
Viewing full declaration
scope information

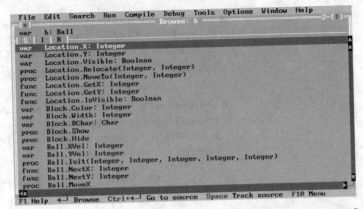

If the ObjectBrowser displays a message telling you a specific symbol isn't found, check to make sure that you have asked the ObjectBrowser to inspect a legitimate symbol or one within the proper scope. For example, you might have your cursor positioned on a comment when you choose Search | Symbol. Or your cursor might be positioned out of the scope in which the ObjectBrowser can find symbol information. For example, your cursor might be on a formal parameter in a function declaration, not in the function implementation. In this case, the ObjectBrowser won't find the symbol, but you find the parameter in the function's implementation, you can browse it.

Reviewing ObjectBrowser functions

Table 4.5 lists the keys and menu commands that activate specific ObjectBrowser functions.

Table 4.5
ObjectBrowser functions

To accomplish this:	Do this:
Browse objects	Choose Search	Objects.
Browse units	Choose Search	Units.
Browse global symbols	Choose Search	Globals.
Browse Symbol	Place your cursor on the symbol in your code, choose Search	Symbol, or hold down *Ctrl* and click the right mouse button.
Select Browser Options	Choose Options	Browser.
Select Source Tracking Options	Choose Options	Environment	Preferences.
Select Mouse Options	Choose Options	Environment	Mouse.

Table 4.5: ObjectBrowser functions (continued)

Open a Previous browser window	Choose Search I Previous Browser, choose Previous on the browser window local menu, or press *Ctrl+P*.
Select Local Browser Options	Press *Ctrl+O*, or choose Options on browser window local menu.
Edit source code	Press *Ctrl+Enter*, press *Ctrl+G*, or choose Goto Source on the browser window local menu.
Track source code	Press *Spacebar* from the ObjectBrowser, press *Ctrl+T*, or choose Track Source on the browser window local menu.
Display reference information	Press *Ctrl+R* from the ObjectBrowser, or click the R in the window frame.
Display scope information	Press *Ctrl+S* from the ObjectBrowser, or click the S in the window frame.
Display inheritance information	Press *Ctrl+I* from the ObjectBrowser, or click the the I in the window frame.
Reverse the current Sub-browsing setting	Hold down *Shift* while you select your next browsing action.

Running other programs from the IDE

You can run other programs and utilities without leaving the IDE. When you install the Borland Pascal package, the IDE is set up to run such programming tools as GREP, Turbo Assembler, Turbo Debugger, and Turbo Profiler.

To run a program from the IDE:

1. Open the Tools menu.

   You'll see the list of programs and utilities you can run.
2. Choose the program you want to run from the Tools menu.

When you choose a program, you transfer control to it. After the program is through running, control is transferred back to the IDE.

Customizing the Tools menu

You can add programs you find useful to the Tools menu and then select them to run from within the IDE.

To add a program to the Tools menu:

1. Choose Options | Tools to display the Tools dialog box.

   In the Program Titles list box, you'll see brief descriptions of the programs already installed and ready to run.

2. Choose New to display the Modify/New Tool dialog box.

3. In the Program Title input box, type the name of the program as you want it to appear on the Tools menu.

   If you want your program to have a keyboard shortcut, type a tilde (~) just before and just after the character you want to be the shortcut. This character will display in bold or in a special color in the Tools menu, and when you press that key, you choose the program. For example, to add Brief to the Tools menu and to make the letter B a keyboard shortcut, type this:

   ```
   ~B~rief
   ```

4. If you want your program to have a hot key associated with it, select one of the Hot Key options. Whenever you press the assigned hot key, the program begins running. For example, hot key *Shift+F2* is assigned to the GREP utility. Any time you want to use GREP, simply press *Shift+F2*.

5. In the Program Path input box, type the program name.

   If you don't enter the full path name, only programs in the current directory or programs in your regular DOS path will be found.

6. In the Command Line input box, type any parameters or macro command you want passed to the program.

   See the Borland Pascal Help system for a complete reference to the macro commands you can use in a Modify/New Tool Command Line box.

7. Choose OK.

To edit an existing Tools menu program:

1. Choose Options | Tools.

2. Select the program you want to edit in the Program Titles list box.

3. Choose Edit.

4. Make your changes to the program title, program path, or command line.

5. Choose OK.

To remove an existing Tools menu program:

1. Choose Options | Tools.
2. Select the program you want to delete.
3. Choose Delete.
4. Choose OK.

Working with the Messages window

Some tools can send program output through a DOS filter, a program that converts the output into a format that can be displayed in the Messages window. See the Help system for more information about using and writing your own DOS filters. One such tool that uses the Messages window is GREP, and its filter is GREP2MSG.EXE. You'll find the source code, GREP2MSG.PAS in the UTILS directory.

When a tool like GREP runs, the Messages window appears and displays the output. You can scroll through the output messages. In the Messages window, you can choose to edit the program line referenced in the message or you can track your messages (highlight one program line after another in your source code as you move through your messages in the Messages window).

To edit the program line referenced in a message,

- If you're using a mouse, double-click the message you're interested in.
- If you're using a keyboard, select the message that references the program line you want to edit and press *Enter*.
- Your cursor jumps to the program line in the source code that is referenced by the message in the Messages window. You can now edit the program line.

The Close On Go To Source option also affects the ObjectBrowser; see page 70.

By default, the Messages window closes when your cursor goes to the program line in the source code. If you prefer that the Messages window remain open, uncheck the Close On Go To Source option in the Preferences dialog box.

To track program lines:

1. In the Messages window, select the message that references the program line you want to track first.
2. Press *Spacebar*.

The Auto Track Source option also affects the ObjectBrowser; see page 70.

If you always want to track your messages in your source code, check Auto Track Source in the Options group of the Preferences dialog box. Then when you scroll through your messages, the referenced program lines are highlighted in your source code automatically; you don't have to press *Spacebar*.

How program lines referenced by messages are tracked depends on how you set tracking options in the Options | Environment | Preferences dialog box: If the referenced file isn't in an edit window, the IDE opens the file and it appears either in a new edit window or in a current edit window.

Source Tracking options also affect the ObjectBrowser and the Integrated debugger.

■ If you want the file to appear in a new edit window, choose New Window as the Source Tracking option.

■ If you want the file to replace the current one in the active edit window, choose Current Window as the Source Tracking option.

If the Messages window has been closed, you can display it again with Tools | Messages.

Configuring the IDE

While writing and editing your programs, you'll probably set editing and preference options, select compiler and linker options, or resize and rearrange your edit windows to your liking. The IDE can remember the settings and files you used during a programming session and use them the next time you start a session.

Saving your working environment

You save your working environment with the Auto Save options: Editor Files, Desktop, and Environment in the Options | Environment | Preferences dialog box.

■ If the Editor Files option is on, the IDE saves all modified files open in edit windows whenever you exit the IDE, choose File | Dos Shell, or run or debug a program.

■ If the Desktop option is on, the IDE saves the name of the files you were working with in a desktop file whenever you exit the IDE, choose File | Dos Shell, or run or debug a program.

■ If the Environment option is on, the IDE saves all editing, compiling, linking, and preference options you selected in a configuration file whenever you exit the IDE, choose File | DOS Shell, or run or debug a program.

Using the configuration file

A configuration file keeps track of all the options set with the Options menu, all the settings selected in the Find Text dialog box, all merged Help files, the target platform, and the name of the primary file, if any. If the Auto Save Environment option is checked in the Options | Environment | Preferences dialog box, each time you exit the IDE, choose File | DOS Shell, or run or debug a program, the current configuration file is updated. The default configuration file name is BP.TP if you're using BP.EXE, or it's TURBO.TP if you're using TURBO.EXE.

To learn how to use a configuration file to manage a programming project, see page 81.

To create a new configuration file for a different project:

1. Choose Options | Save As.
2. Type a new name in the Options File Name input box.
3. Choose OK.

To change to another existing configuration file:

1. Choose Options | Open.
2. Specify the name of an existing configuration file.
3. Choose OK.

To modify your existing configuration:

1. Change the options you want.
2. Choose Options | Save.

   The IDE saves all your changes in the current configuration file.

Using the desktop file

If you check the Auto Save Desktop option in the Options | Environment | Preferences dialog box, the IDE updates a *desktop file* each time you exit the IDE, choose File | DOS Shell, or run or debug a program. A desktop file keeps track of the files you opened and the files you worked on but closed during a programming session (except NONAMExx.PAS files). When you start a new session, your edit windows appear just as you left them. When you open the File menu, you see a list of closed files that you opened earlier. As long as you use the same desktop file, the list of closed files on the File menu continues to grow, up to a maximum of five files.

How do you determine which desktop file to use? You can't select a new desktop file directly, but every time you create a new configuration file, the IDE creates a new desktop file. The file name is the same, except a desktop file has a .DSK extension instead of a .TP extension. For example, if your configuration file is named MY.TP, then the desktop file is MY.DSK.

By default, the IDE saves a desktop file in the same directory as the current configuration file. If you prefer, you can choose to save desktop files in the current directory:

1. Choose Options | Environment | Preferences.
2. In the Desktop File group, select Current Directory.

At times you might want to keep your current configuration settings but clear your desktop so the IDE "forgets" the list of files you have been working with, clears all history lists, and closes all windows. Do this:

1. Choose Options | Environment | Preferences.
2. In the Preferences dialog box, make sure Desktop is on and Environment is off.
3. Choose File | Exit to exit the IDE.
4. Restart the IDE.

   The IDE closes all your windows and remembers your current settings, but your desktop, history lists, and closed files list are cleared.

Preserving symbols across sessions

You can choose to save symbol information in a symbol file (a file with a .PSM extension) at the same time you save a desktop file. Then the next time you start the IDE, the symbol information generated during your last compilation will be available to you so that you can immediately browse and debug.

To preserve symbols across sessions:

1. Choose Options | Environment | Preferences.
2. Check to be sure the Auto Save Desktop option is on.
3. In the Desktop File Options group, select Desktop and Symbols.
4. Choose OK.

Managing a project

If you want to make your programming project modular and easier to control, use a *primary file*. Specify your main program file as the primary file and have it use several unit or Include files where you keep large chunks of your code.

To specify which file is your primary file, follow these steps:

1. Choose Compile | Primary File.
2. When the dialog box appears, type the name of your file or select it from the Files list box.
3. Choose OK.

Now when you use Compile | Make or Build, the primary file compiles, even if it's not the file in your active edit window.

Each project you work on in the IDE has unique requirements. For example, each project has a different primary file and different directories where your files are located. You can customize the IDE to your project.

Manage multiple projects with a configuration file for each.

The secret to project management in the IDE is to use a different configuration file for each project. When you begin a new project, create a new configuration file:

1. Set all options the way you want them to be for the new project.
2. Specify a primary file.
3. Use Options | Directories to specify the directories where the compiler looks to find your files for this project.
4. Choose Save As from the Options menu.

   A dialog box prompts you for a new configuration file name.
5. Specify a new configuration file name.
6. Choose OK.

If you exit the IDE at this point and the Auto Save Desktop and Environment options are on (Options | Environment | Preferences), the IDE uses the new configuration and desktop files the next time you start a new session. The files you were working with will be readily available to you, either in an edit window or in the closed files listing on the File menu, because a new desktop file has also been created for your project.

☞ If you keep each of your Pascal projects in separate directories, here is a tip to make managing a project more convenient. When you have set all the options as you want them to be for the project and specified a primary file, if any, do this:

1. Choose Save As from the Options menu.
2. Specify a new configuration file name including the full path the project directory.

   ■ If you're using BP.EXE, specify BP.TP as the new configuration file name.
   ■ If you're using TURBO.EXE, specify TURBO.TP as the new configuration file name.

3. Choose OK.

   By saving BP.TP or TURBO.TP in the project's directory, you can go to the project directory, start the IDE, and the IDE automatically loads the configuration file in that directory.

If you no longer want a file specified as a primary file, you can use two methods to *clear* a primary file:

■ Choose Compile | Clear Primary File.
■ Choose Primary File and choose Clear in the Primary File dialog box.

If you want to work on a different project, load the new project's configuration file with Options | Open.

5

Programming in the Windows IDE

The Windows IDE can create Windows, DOS real-mode, and DOS protected-mode applications.

The Windows IDE is very similar to Borland Pascal's DOS IDEs. Most of the functions you perform in the DOS IDEs are performed the same way in the Windows IDE. If you haven't read the previous chapter, "Programming in a DOS IDE," take the time to do so now.

This chapter points out the unique features of the Windows IDE and explains the slight differences between the Windows and the DOS IDEs.

Because Borland Pascal for Windows runs under Windows, we assume you have knowledge about using Windows. If you are comfortable with Windows, you'll be comfortable with the Borland Pascal for Windows IDE as well.

Starting the Windows IDE

To start the Windows IDE, double-click the Borland Pascal for Windows icon in the Program Manager, or select it with your keyboard and press *Enter*.

You can also start the Windows IDE from the DOS prompt. Type

```
WIN BPW
```

Going one step further, at the DOS prompt you can also specify which files to open in edit windows and which configuration file to use. Here's the syntax to use:

WIN BPW [/CConfig file] files

For example, the following line starts up Windows, begins running the Windows IDE using the settings in the MYCONFIG.CFG file, and opens two windows, one containing MYFILE.PAS and the other holding YOURFILE.INC:

```
WIN BPW /Cmyconfig myfile yourfile
```

Using the SpeedBar

With the IDE's SpeedBar and a mouse, you can quickly choose menu commands and other actions.

The buttons on the SpeedBar represent menu commands. They are shortcuts for your mouse, just as certain key combinations are shortcuts when you use your keyboard. To choose a command, click a button with your mouse. If you click the Open a File button, for example, the IDE responds just as if you chose the Open command on the File menu.

The SpeedBar is context-sensitive. Which buttons appear on it depend on which is your active window: the desktop window or an edit window.

The desktop window SpeedBar appears when you have no edit windows open in the IDE. These buttons appear on the desktop window SpeedBar:

Figure 5.1
Buttons on the desktop
window SpeedBar

Help system Contents screen   Make

Open a file   Make and run

Exit the IDE   Make and run under Turbo
Debugger

These buttons appear on the edit window SpeedBar:

Figure 5.2
Buttons on the edit window
SpeedBar

Help on the editor

Paste from Clipboard

Open a file

Undo

Save a file

Compile

Search for text

Make

Search again

Make and run

Cut to Clipboard

Make and run under Turbo
Debugger

Copy to Clipboard

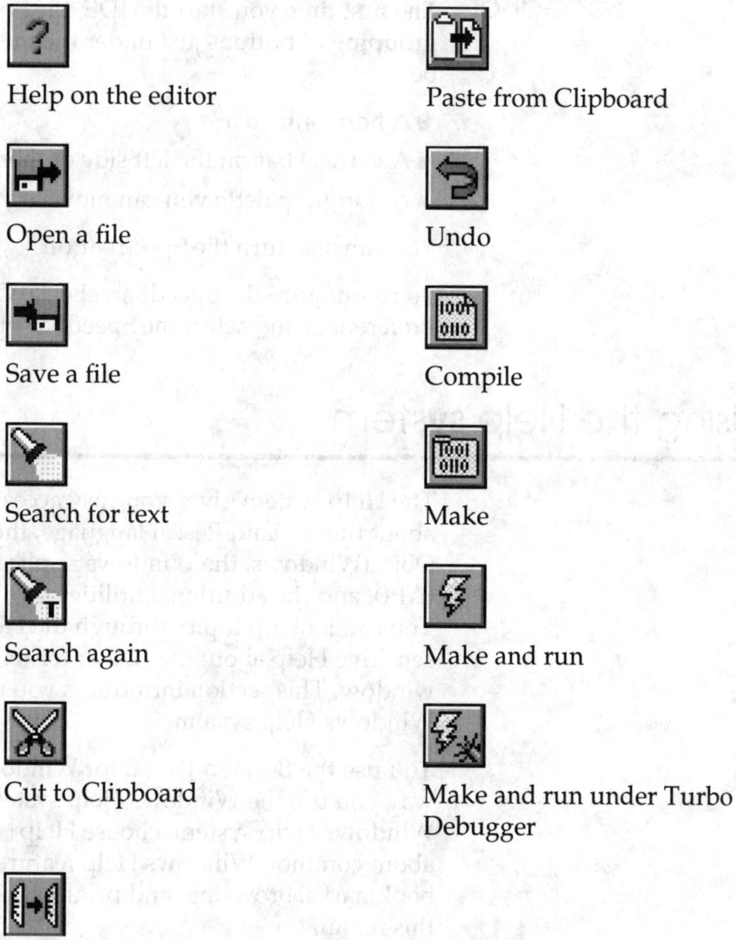

Some of the buttons on the SpeedBar are dimmed at times. This means that the command the button represents is not available to you in the current context. For example, if an edit window is open and the Clipboard is empty, the Paste Text from Clipboard button is dimmed.

Configuring the SpeedBar

The first time you start the IDE, the SpeedBar is a horizontal grouping of buttons just under the menu bar. The SpeedBar can be

- A horizontal bar
- A vertical bar on the left side of the IDE desktop
- A pop-up palette you can move anywhere on your desktop

You can also turn the SpeedBar off.

To reconfigure the SpeedBar, choose Options | Environment | Preferences and select the SpeedBar option you want.

Using the Help system

The Help system gives you easy access to detailed information about the Borland Pascal language, the IDE, the run-time library, ObjectWindows, the Windows application programming interface (API), and the additional utilities provided with Borland Pascal. You can look up topics through the Help window, or get context-sensitive Help about the IDE or terms you have typed into an edit window. This section introduces you to the Borland Pascal for Windows Help system.

You use the Borland Pascal for Windows Help system the same way you use the Windows Help system. To learn how to use the Windows Help system, choose Help | Using Help. You'll find out about common Windows Help features (such as annotating, using bookmarks, browsing, and printing) that are not mentioned in this manual.

The following sections explain the many ways you can use the Borland Pascal for Windows Help system while you are developing your applications in the IDE.

To learn more about using Help, choose Help | Using Help or press *F1* from anywhere in the Help system.

Moving around in the Help system

When you look at Help screens, you see underlined text colored differently than the surrounding text. These are *links*. Links are text, icons, or graphics that you can select to get more information. You can use links to display a new Help screen that presents new information on the topic underlined; choose one of two ways:

- Click the link.
- Press *Tab* repeatedly until the link is highlighted, then press *Enter*.

A new Help screen appears with information on the topic you selected: You have "jumped" to a new location in the Help system. You might see more links on this screen, which you can select for even more information.

To return to a previous Help screen, choose one of two ways:

Choose the Back button to return to your most recent screen.

You might also see text underlined with a dotted line colored differently than the surrounding text. You can use this type of link to display a pop-up window with more information. Try one of these ways:

Choose the History button to see a list of your most recent screens. From this list, choose the Help screen you want to see.

- Click the text.
- Press *Tab* repeatedly until the topic you want is highlighted, then press *Enter*.

A pop-up window appears containing information on the topic you selected. It remains on your screen until you click your mouse button or press the *Enter* key. When the window is gone, you'll still be in the same place in the Help system.

Asking for Help

You can access Help several ways:

- Click Help on the Menu bar or press *Alt+H* to display the Help menu.

  The IDE displays its Help menu. From this menu, you can choose to see a Contents screen for the entire Help system, get Help on using the Help system, display information on the topic your cursor is resting on in the active edit window, or display Borland Pascal-specific information such as language help, Borland Pascal error messages, example programs, and so on.

■ Press *Shift+F1* to display the Borland Pascal Help Contents screen.

You can click the icons on the Contents screen to display Help information.

The Contents screen is very similar to a table of contents in a book, but instead of turning to a page to see information about a topic, you choose a topic by either clicking the underlined topic or by pressing *Tab* to reach the topic and then pressing *Enter*.

■ Press *F1*.

- If you're in an edit window, a Help screen appears with information about using the editor. Choose any of the jumps for more details.

- If a menu option is selected, a context-sensitive Help screen appears with information about that menu item.

■ Choose the Help button from within a dialog box.

A screen appears with brief explanations about all the options available to you in the dialog box. If you click an underlined topic or select it with your keyboard and press *Enter*, you see more detail about your selected option.

■ Place your cursor on a keyword in an edit window and choose Topic Search. You can choose from four methods:

- Press *Ctrl+F1*.

- Choose Help I Topic Search.

- Hold down the *Ctrl* key and click your right mouse button. (You must have customized your right mouse button first—choose Options I Environment I Mouse and check the Topic Search option.)

To learn about local menus see page 49.

- Choose Search for Topic on the edit window local menu.

A Help screen appears displaying information about the keyword your cursor is on in the active edit window.

■ From any Help screen window, choose the Search button.

If you know what you are looking for, the Search button is the quickest way to display the Help screen you want.

A Search dialog box appears. In its top list box, you can scroll through every topic in the Borland Pascal Help system. If you know the topic you are searching for, begin typing the topic in the input box and you'll see the topic you want displayed in the list box. Select the topic and choose Show Topics.

If your topic is broken down into more detail, you'll see more topics in the bottom list box. Select the topic you want and choose Go To. The Help screen for your topic appears.

- Choose the Help icon on the SpeedBar.

The editor Help screen appears.

Copying code examples

The Help system has a code example for each procedure and function. You can copy these examples from the Help system into your edit window. To copy an example,

1. Display the Help screen for a procedure or function you are interested in.

   You'll see the name of a sample code example at the bottom of the Help screen.

2. Click the name of the sample code to display it.

3. Choose Edit | Copy.

   A dialog box appears that displays the sample code. You may select a portion of the code to copy to the Clipboard. If you don't, the entire code sample will be copied.

4. Choose Copy.

5. Return to your edit window and choose Edit | Paste, press *Shift+Ins*, or click the Paste from Clipboard button on the SpeedBar.

Exiting Help

You can choose to keep a Help screen displayed when you return to the IDE, or you can close the main Help window altogether.

- To return to your program and keep the current Help window in the background, click the window you wish to make active. Click the Help window when you want to bring it to the foreground and make it the active window again.

- To close the main Help window and return to your application, select File | Exit from the Help window menu or double-click its Control menu button.

Writing and editing your code

The editor lets you open up to 32 edit windows at a time, memory allowing.

Because the IDE editor behaves like other Windows editors, you probably know how to edit text already. The editor follows Common User Access (CUA) guidelines, the standard used by most Windows programs. The same editing commands you use in other Windows applications work in the IDE editor as well. You'll find a complete editor reference in Appendix A in the *Programmer's Reference*.

Configuring the editor

You have several options to modify the behavior of the editor. Choose Options | Environment | Editor to display the Editor dialog box.

For information about syntax highlighting in the editor, see page 91.

To find out more about each option, select the option and choose Help or press *F1*. The Help system explains what the option does.

Command sets

To decide which command set to use, see Appendix A of the Programmer's Reference or use Help.

Both sources list all the editing commands in the two command sets.

The Windows IDE editor has two command sets: the CUA command set that makes the editor behave like other Windows editors, and the Alternate command set that turns the editor into a Borland-style editor. In addition, many commands are available in both command sets.

When you start up the Windows IDE for the first time, the editor uses the CUA command set. It supports all the editing commands common to Windows programs and many of the editing commands long-time Borland language users expect in a Borland product.

To use the Alternate command set, choose Options | Environment | Preferences and select the Alternate option from the Command Set group.

The command set you choose affects more than just the editor. For example, some menu commands have hot keys, which are keys you can press to choose the command without using the menu. In the Alternate command set, *F2* is a quick way to save a file. There is no hot key for saving a file in the CUA command set. Hot keys are listed to the right of menu commands.

Using the editor

The same editor is in the DOS and Windows IDEs. Once you know how to use it in one IDE, you'll be able to use it in the other. To learn about undoing mistakes, working with blocks of text, searching for text and delimiters, and positioning your cursor on a specific line number, read pages 44 to 49 in the previous chapter, "Programming in a DOS IDE."

There are two small differences between the Windows and the DOS editors:

- The Windows editor doesn't have the Find Text at Cursor option.
- The Windows editor doesn't have the Block Insert Cursor option to make the cursor a block cursor when insert mode is on.

Syntax highlighting

The Windows IDE also has syntax highlighting. You can color elements of your code just as you can in a DOS IDE, but you can also change the attributes of the text. For example, you can boldface, italicize, and underline code elements as well as color them.

To display the Highlighting dialog box, choose Options | Environment | Highlight.

Figure 5.3
Highlighting dialog box

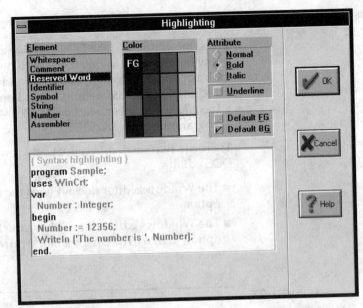

The list box on the left lists the elements of Pascal code.

Coloring your text   To change the color of an element, follow these steps:

1. Select the element you want to change in the Element list box.
2. Select the colors you want in the Colors matrix.

   The current foreground color is marked with the letters FG; the current background color is marked with the letters BG. If the foreground and background colors are the same, the letters FB appear on the color square.

   ■ To select a foreground color with your mouse, click it. To select the color with your keyboard, press *Tab* until the Color matrix is selected, use the arrow keys to move around the Color matrix, and when you're on the color of your choice, press *F*.

   ■ To select a background color with your mouse, click it with the right mouse button. To select the color with your keyboard, press *Tab* until the Color matrix is selected, use the arrow keys to move around the Color matrix, and when you're on the color of your choice, press *B*.

   When you select a color, the results are reflected in the sample code.

3. Choose OK.

Using the Windows system colors

Windows uses a window background color and a text color, and most Windows applications use these same colors. To change the Windows system colors, use the Control Panel in the Program Manager.

You can choose to use the Windows system colors in the IDE's editor. To use the Windows system foreground color for an element, follow these steps:

1. From the Highlighting dialog box, select the element in the Elements list box.
2. Select the Default FG option.

Follow the same steps to change the background color, except select the Default BG option.

Changing text attributes

To boldface or italicize text, the editor must use a fixed pitch or monospaced font.

To change fonts, choose Options I Environment I Editor and select the Font option you want.

To select the attribute of an element, follow these steps:

1. From the Highlighting dialog box, select the element in the Element list box.
2. Select the attribute from the Attributes options.

When you make an attribute selection, you'll see it reflected in the sample code window.

☞ You can also select an element to change by clicking an occurrence of it in the sample code window. For example, if you click the reserved word **program**, the element Reserved Word is selected in the Element list box. Changing colors or attributes changes all the reserved words in the sample code.

Printin your code

When you want a printed copy of your code, choose File I Print. The editor expands tabs (replaces tab characters with the appropriate number of spaces) and then prints your file.

Syntax highlighting printing

You can print your text so that syntax elements are highlighted:

1. Choose File I Printer Setup.
2. Check the Syntax Printing option.
3. Choose OK.

4. Choose File | Print to print your text.

If Syntax Highlight is on, elements of your printed text will be highlighted.

For details about configuring a printer in Windows, see your Microsoft Windows User's Guide.

When you installed Windows on your system, you probably also installed one or more printer drivers so you could print from Windows. The File | Printer Setup command lets you select which printer you want to use for printing from the IDE and how you want it configured. For example, you might want to print on a different size paper. You can set your printer up to do this from within the IDE by choosing the Set Up button in the Printer Setup dialog box.

Working with files

As you program in the IDE, you create new files, open existing ones, and save them. Table 2.1 summarizes the basic file-management tasks:

Table 5.1
File operations

Operation	Description
File	New	Opens a new edit window and gives it a temporary name
File	Open	Opens an existing file or creates a new one with a name you specify
File	Save	Saves the file in the active edit window to disk
File	Save As	Saves the file in the active edit window under a different name
File	Save All	Saves all modified files

Opening files

To open a file, follow these steps:

1. Choose File | Open or choose the Open a File button on the SpeedBar and the File Open dialog box appears. You can then take any of the following actions to specify a file to open:

   ■ Type a full file name in the input box.

   ■ Type a file name with wildcards. This filters the Files list to match your file specification. In the Files list, select the file name you want to edit.

- Click the ↓ to display a history list of file specifications or file names you entered earlier. Select the file name or specification you want. Selecting a file specification displays files that match that specification.
- View the contents of other directories by double-clicking a directory name in the file list. Select the name of the file you want to edit.

2. Choose OK.

You can also just press *Enter* once the file is selected, or simply double-click the name of the file you want when you see it listed, and the file opens.

If you open one or more files and then close them, you'll see them listed at the bottom of the File menu, up to a maximum of five files. If you select one of these file names on the menu, the file opens in an edit window. When you work with many open files, you can close some, yet open them again quickly using the list and reduce clutter on your desktop.

Where are my files?

If this is your first attempt at programming under Windows, you might be confused about where the IDE looks for and saves your files. The IDE uses the *current work directory*. This list explains how the current work directory is determined:

For more about primary files, see page 81.

- If you specify a primary file, the directory it is in becomes the current work directory. You can include a full path name when naming a primary file.
- If you didn't specify a primary file, the directory that contains the file in the active edit window becomes the current work directory. You can include a full path name when saving a file in an edit window.
- If there is no active edit window, the directory BPW.EXE is in becomes the current work directory.

Once you open or create a file, Borland Pascal remembers its full path even if the current work directory changes.

To learn how to save your working environment, see page 78.

Because the current work directory is usually determined either by the primary file or by the file in the active edit window, and these items are saved in the configuration and desktop files, the configuration and desktop files indirectly determine the current work directory for a project.

Working with files in another directory

To open a file in another directory, choose File | Open and type the complete path and file name in the input box. Or you can use the directory list to display files in another directory and select the file you want. Once you specify a file name and choose *Enter*, the next time you choose File | Open in the same session, you will see the files in this other directory. Your current work directory has not changed, however. If you create and save a new file, the IDE saves it in the current work directory.

If you want to work with files in more than one directory, you can use the history list in the File Open dialog box. Click the drop-down arrow to the right of the input box or press *Alt+↓* to see the history list; you might see the file you want listed.

Compiling and running

You compile and run programs in the Windows IDE the same way you would in the DOS IDEs. Read about compiling and running programs within an IDE on page 54. You should note these points, however:

- If your program uses the *WinCrt* unit, the program's window becomes *inactive* when the program stops running. Close it to continue working in the IDE.

  To prevent the user from having to close the *WinCrt* window, use the *DoneWinCrt* procedure. Look up *DoneWinCrt* in Chapter 1 of the the *Programmer's Reference*.

- If an error occurs in a program that uses the *WinCrt* unit while the program is running, the window the program runs in becomes inactive *before* the program finishes. To find out what happened, close the program window. Then you'll see an information box displaying the error number and the memory address where the error occurred.

Browsing through your code

The Windows IDE has a new programming tool, the Object-Browser. It lets you explore the objects and units in your programs and much more. Even if the applications you develop don't use object-oriented programming, you'll still find the Object-Browser an extremely valuable tool. Taking full advantage of the Windows graphical environment, the ObjectBrowser lets you browse through your object hierarchies, units, and all the procedures, functions, variables, types, constants, and labels your program uses. With the ObjectBrowser, you can do these things:

- Graphically view the object hierarchies in your application, then select the object of your choice and view the procedures, functions, and other symbols it contains.
- List the global symbols your program uses, then select one and view its declaration, list all references to it in your program, or go to where it is declared in your source code.
- List all the units your program uses, then select one and list all the symbols in its interface part. From this list, you can select a symbol and browse as you would with any other symbol in your program.
- Select a symbol in your source code, then view its details at the click of the right mouse button.

☞ Before you use the ObjectBrowser, be sure to check these options in the Options | Compiler dialog box:

- Debug Information
- Local Symbols
- Symbol Information

To activate the ObjectBrowser, choose Objects, Units, or Globals on the Search menu. You can also place your cursor on a symbol in your code and choose Search | Symbol to bring up the Object-Browser. If the program in the current window or the primary file hasn't been compiled yet, you'll see the IDE compile your program before a browser window appears.

☞ If your program compiles, makes, or builds successfully once, you make some changes to your code, and your next compilation fails, you can still browse through your application as it existed at the last successful compilation. For this to happen, the Preserve Symbols startup option must be on; this is the default setting. Find this option in the Options | Environment | Startup dialog box. Because Preserve Symbols is a startup option, if you check or uncheck this option, the new setting won't take effect until you exit the IDE and then restart it again.

You can also choose Browse Symbol at Cursor from the edit window local menu to quickly browse the symbol your cursor is resting on in your code.

If you have a mouse, you'll find browsing through your code more convenient if you set up your right mouse button to activate the ObjectBrowser. Then you can hold down the *Ctrl* key while you use your right mouse button to click an object, procedure, function, variable, or other symbol in your source code and inspect it (view its details).

To set up your mouse for browsing, follow these steps:

1. Choose Options | Environment | Mouse.
2. Select Browse as the Ctrl + Right Mouse Button option.
3. Choose OK.

The ObjectBrowser has a SpeedBar at the top of the Object-Browser window. Choose any SpeedBar button by clicking it with your mouse or using a hot key. By choosing a button or an associated hot key, you tell the ObjectBrowser to perform some action. These are the buttons you will see, their keyboard equivalents, and the action they perform:

*Figure 5.4
Buttons on the
ObjectBrowser SpeedBar*

F1   Help

Ctrl+G   Go to the source code for the selected item

Exactly which buttons appear on the SpeedBar depends on which Object-Browser window you are working with.
Ctrl+B   Browse (view the details of) the selected item

Ctrl+V   View the previous browser window

Ctrl+O   Display an overview of the object hierarchy

User's Guide

Ctrl+R   List all references of a symbol

Ctrl+P   Print the object hierarchy

Ctrl+W   Replace current browser window

Ctrl+W   Open a new browser window

The last two buttons shown are actually two different views of the same button. The first time you use the ObjectBrowser, you'll see the Single Window button. Click it and it is replaced with the Multiple Window button.

When you choose the Single Window button and begin browsing, a new browser window replaces the previous window each time you perform a new browsing action. When you choose the Multiple Window button, windows remain onscreen until you close them.

You can quickly reverse the action of the Window buttons; hold down *Shift* as you select your next browse action. For example, if the Multiple Window button is displayed, when you hold down *Shift*, the next browser window you open replaces the current one.

Browsing through objects

The ObjectBrowser lets you see the "big picture," the object hierarchies in your application, as well as the small details. To activate the ObjectBrowser and see your objects displayed graphically, choose Search | Objects. The ObjectBrowser draws your objects and shows their ancestor-descendant relationships in a horizontal tree. The red lines in the hierarchy help you see the immediate ancestor-descendant relationships of the currently selected object more clearly.

Figure 5.5
Viewing the object hierarchy
of an application

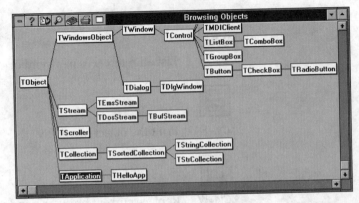

To see more detail about a particular object, double-click it. If you aren't using a mouse, select the object by using your arrow cursor keys and press *Enter*. The ObjectBrowser lists the symbols (the procedures, functions, variables, and so on) used in the object.

Figure 5.6
Viewing the details of an
object

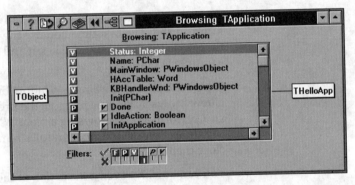

One or more letters appear to the left of each symbol in the object. The letters describe what kind of symbol it is.

Table 5.2
Letter symbols in the
ObjectBrowser

Letter	Symbol
F	Function
P	Procedure
T	Type
V	Variable
C	Constant
L	Label
I	Inherited from an ancestor
p	Private symbol
v	Virtual method

User's Guide

Filters

The same letters that identify the kind of symbol appear in a Filters matrix at the bottom of the ObjectBrowser window. You can use filters to select the type of symbols you want to see listed.

You can also use the Browser Options dialog box to select the type of symbols. Choose Options | Browser and select the symbols you want to see listed.

The Filters matrix has a column for each letter; the letter can appear in the top or bottom row of this column.

To view all instances of a particular type of symbol, click the top cell of the letter's column. For example, to view all the variables in the currently selected object, click the top cell in the **V** column. All the variables used in the object appear.

You can change several filter settings at once. Drag your mouse over the cells you want to select in the Filters matrix.

To hide all instances of a particular type of symbol, click the bottom cell of the letter's column. For example, to view only the functions and procedures in an object, you need to hide all the variables. Click the bottom cell in the **V** column, and click the top cells in the **F** and **P** columns.

In some cases more than one letter appears next to a symbol. The second letter appears just after the letter identifying the type of symbol and further describes the symbol:

- **I** indicates an inherited symbol
- *p* indicates a private symbol
- *v* indicates a virtual symbol

Viewing declarations of listed symbols

Use one of these methods to see the declaration of a particular listed symbol:

- Double-click the symbol.
- Select the symbol and click the Browse button or press *Ctrl+B*.
- Select the symbol and press *Enter*.

If you are browsing in single-window mode (the Window button displays only one window on the SpeedBar), and you want to return to a higher level, click the Previous Browser Window button or press *Ctrl+V*.

Although it's very easy to use the SpeedBar to choose between single- and multiple-window mode, you can do the same thing using menus and a dialog box also. To have a new browser window replace the current one:

1. Choose Options | Browser.
2. Check the Replace Current sub-browsing option.

3. Choose OK.

To have the current browser window remain when you select a
symbol listed in it to browse:

1. Choose Options | Browser.
2. Check the New Browser sub-browsing option.
3. Choose OK.

Browsing through global symbols

Choose Search | Globals to open a window that lists every global
symbol in your application in alphabetical order.

Click the symbol you want more information about or use your
cursor keys to select it. A Search input box at the bottom of the
window lets you quickly search through the list of global symbols
by typing the first few letters of the symbol's name. As you type,
the highlight bar in the list box moves to a symbol that matches
the typed characters.

Once you select the global symbol you are interested in, you can

■ Choose the Browse button to see the declaration of the symbol.
■ Choose the Go To Source Code button to see how the symbol is
  declared in the source code.
■ Choose the Reference button to see a list of references to the
  symbol. To go to the actual reference in the code, double-click
  the reference in the reference list, or select it and press *Enter*.

Browsing through units

With the ObjectBrowser, you can browse through all the units
your program uses. Choose Search | Units to open a window that
lists all the units in your program and the application name itself.

Select the unit you want more information about. Just as you can
with global symbols, you can search through the unit list by
typing the first few letters of the unit name in the Search input
box at the bottom of the window.

Once you have selected the unit, you can list all the symbols in the
interface part of the unit:

■ In the displayed list of units, double-click the unit name, select the unit name and choose Inspect, or select the name and press *Enter*.

From this list, you can select a symbol and do these things:

• To see the symbol's declaration, double-click the symbol, select it, and choose the Inspect button, or select it and press *Enter*.

• To go to the line in the source code where the symbol is declared, choose the Go To Source Code button.

• To list all references to the symbol, choose the Reference button. If you choose one of these references, the Object-Browser positions your cursor at that reference in your source code.

■ To go to the symbol's declaration in your source code, choose the Go to Source Code button.

■ To list all references to the symbol in your application, choose the Reference button.

Browsing symbols in your code

You can also browse any symbol in your code without viewing object hierarchies or lists of symbols first. Choose from these methods:

■ Highlight the symbol in your code and choose Search | Symbol.

■ If your mouse is configured for browsing, hold down the *Ctrl* key and click the symbol in your code with the right mouse button.

■ Click the right mouse button or press *Alt+F10* to display the local edit window menu and choose Browse at Symbol.

If the symbol you select to browse is a structured type, the Object-Browser shows you all the symbols in the scope of that type. You can then choose to inspect any of these further. For example, if you choose an object type, you'll see all the symbols listed that are within the scope of the object.

Running other programs from the IDE

You have the choice of running four other programs from within the IDE: Turbo Debugger, Resource Workshop, WinSight, and

Turbo Profiler. To run any of these, choose Tools to open the Tools menu and choose the tool you want to run. To change the path for, or to pass arguments to one of these programs, use the Tools dialog box (Options | Tools).

Unlike the DOS IDEs, you can't add other utilities and programs to the Tools menu. Because the Windows IDE is a Windows application, this is not really a disadvantage. You can always switch to another program using Windows task-switching capabilities.

Configuring the IDE

You configure the IDE, save your working environment, and manage projects much the same way you do in the DOS IDEs. See pages 78 to 82 for details. These are differences between the DOS and Windows IDEs when saving your environment and managing projects:

- The Windows IDE always saves the desktop file in the same directory as the current configuration file. You can't change this as you can in the DOS IDEs.
- To clear a primary file, choose Compile | Clear Primary File in the Windows IDE. You can use this method in the DOS IDEs too, but you also have the option of choosing the Clear Primary File button in the Primary File dialog box.

6

Debugging in the IDE

The Borland Pascal integrated development environment (IDE) includes a number of features to facilitate program development: automatic project management, program modularity, high-speed compilation, and easy-to-use overlays. But with all that, your program can still have *bugs*, or errors, that keep it from working correctly.

Borland Pascal's DOS IDEs give you tools for *debugging* your programs; that is, finding and removing the errors. This chapter outlines the tools and procedures for debugging your programs in the IDE, including the following topics:

- Overview of bugs and debugging
- Controlling program execution
- Watching program output
- Examining values
- Breaking into an executing program

This chapter applies to the integrated debugger in the DOS IDEs. All the tasks described also apply to Turbo Debugger and Turbo Debugger for Windows, although menu names and keystrokes vary.

What is debugging?

Debugging is the process of locating and fixing program errors that prevent your programs from operating correctly. Before we delve into the specific tools in the Borland Pascal IDE that help you in debugging, here's an overview of the kinds of bugs you might be looking for and the kinds of operations you'll be using to find them.

What kinds of bugs are there?

There are three basic kinds of program bugs: compile-time errors, run-time errors, and logic errors. If you already have a good grasp of those concepts, you can skip to the next section on debugging techniques.

Compile-time errors

Compile-time errors, or *syntax* errors, occur when your code violates a rule of Pascal syntax. Borland Pascal can't compile your program unless the program contains valid Pascal statements. When the compiler comes to a statement it can't understand, it stops compiling, brings the offending file into an editor window, positions the cursor at the spot it doesn't understand, and displays an error message.

The command-line compiler also gives the same kind of information. When it finds a syntax error, it displays the line containing the error, with the line number and error message.

The most common causes of compile-time errors are typographical errors, omitted semicolons, references to variables that haven't been declared, passing the wrong number (or type) of parameters to a procedure or function, and assigning values of the wrong type to a variable.

After you correct the error, you can restart the compilation. Once you have eliminated all the syntax errors and your program compiles successfully, you are ready to run the program and look for run-time errors and logic errors.

Run-time errors

Run-time errors, or *semantic* errors, happen when you compile a complete program that does something illegal when you execute it. That is, the program contains legal Pascal statements, but executing the statements does something wrong. For example, your program might be trying to open a nonexistent file for input or to divide by zero.

When a Borland Pascal program encounters such an error, it terminates and prints a message like this:

```
Run-time error ## at seg:ofs
```

If you're running the program from the IDE, Borland Pascal automatically locates the statement that caused the error, just as it does with syntax errors. If you're running the program outside the IDE, you can start the IDE and use Search | Find Error, giving it the seg:ofs address, to locate the statement that caused the error. If you're using the command-line compiler, you can use the /**F** option to find the error.

Logic errors

Logic errors are errors in design and implementation. That is, your Pascal statements are perfectly valid and they do *something*, but what they do is not what you intended. These errors are often hard to track down, because the IDE can't find them automatically as it can with syntax and semantic errors. Fortunately the IDE includes debugging features that can help you locate logic errors.

Logic errors are to blame when variables have incorrect or unexpected values, graphic images don't look right, or code isn't executed when you expect it. The rest of this chapter discusses techniques for tracking down these logic errors.

Debugging techniques

Sometimes when a program does something you didn't expect, the reason is readily apparent, and you can quickly correct the code. But other errors are more subtle or involve interactions with different parts of the program. In these cases, it is most helpful to stop your program at a given point, walk through it step-by-step, and look at the state of variables and expressions. This controlled execution is the key to debugging.

This section briefly describes the various debugging capabilities of the Borland Pascal DOS IDEs.

Stepping and tracing	The Step Over and Trace Into options on the Run menu give you the ability to execute your program one line at a time. The only difference between stepping and tracing is the way they deal with procedure and function calls. Stepping over a procedure or function treats the call as a simple statement, and returns control to you at the next line, after the subprogram finishes. Tracing into the routine loads the code for that routine and continues stepping through it line-by-line.
Breaking	There are two ways to tell the IDE to run your program to a certain point and then stop. The first and simplest way is to locate the position in your program where you want to stop, then choose Go to Cursor from the Run menu. Your program executes as usual until it reaches the statement where you told it to stop, at which point you can examine values and continue running either continuously or step-by-step.
	The second way to stop your program at a certain point is to set a *breakpoint* where you want the program to stop. When you run the program, it stops before executing the statement at the breakpoint. Breakpoints are more flexible than using the Go to Cursor method because you can have several breakpoints throughout your program.
Watching and modifying	While you step through a program, you can watch the program output in several ways. The first is to swap screens as needed. The second is to use a second monitor. Third, you can open a window in the DOS IDE that holds the program's output.
	In addition to showing program output, the integrated debugger lets you watch the values of variables, expressions, and data structures. You can add or remove items to watch in the Watches window using the Watches command in the Debug menu.
	If you want to change the value of a variable, rather than just watch it, you can bring up a dialog box using the Evaluate/Modify command on the Debug menu. In that dialog box, you can examine variables and expressions and change the values of any variables, including strings, pointers, array elements, and record fields, to test how your code reacts to different conditions.

Finding   If you need to find procedure and function declarations or object definitions in your code, you can locate them easily with the ObjectBrowser. Bring up the appropriate browser window using the Search menu and choose Objects, Globals, Units, or Symbols. See page 64 in Chapter 4, "Programming in a DOS IDE" for more about browsing through your code.

While tracing, you can scroll back through the function calls that got you to where you are by looking at the Call Stack window (Debug | Call Stack). This window shows each procedure and function call along with its parameters.

Generating debugging information

Before you can debug a program, you have to tell the compiler to generate some extra information so it can keep track of which lines in your source code correspond to particular parts of the executing program. This extra information is called *debugging information*. You turn it on by either checking the appropriate box in the IDE's Compiler Options (Options | Compiler) dialog box or by inserting a compiler directive into your code.

When you compile a Borland Pascal program, the compiler always keeps a list of the identifiers used, called the *symbol table*. This list tracks all variables, constants, types, and procedure and function names. For debugging purposes, it also has to track line numbers in your source code files for all these identifiers. By checking Debug Information in the Compiler Options dialog box or by using the **$D+** compiler directive, you tell the compiler to add line-number information to the symbol table.

Integrated vs. standalone   In the Debugger Options (Options | Debugger) dialog box, you can tell the compiler whether to generate debugging information for use in the integrated debugger, for use by a standalone debugger such as Turbo Debugger, or for both. The Integrated option, which is checked by default, must be checked if you want to use the integrated debugger.

Information in units   If you're writing a large program that uses units and your debugging information gets too large, you can cut down the amount of information generated for particular units by using the **$L-** compiler directive in individual units, or by unchecking Local Symbols in the Compiler Options dialog box.

If you turn off the generation of information on a unit's local symbols, debugging information for that unit excludes all identifiers declared in the unit's implementation section. Full information is still generated for all identifiers in the interface section, so you can still debug using those.

Controlling execution

The most basic part of using the integrated debugger is controlling execution. By managing the stage when each instruction is executed, you can more easily determine which part of your program is causing a problem. The debugger provides five basic tools for controlling the execution of a program, enabling you to

- Step through instructions
- Trace into instructions
- Run to a certain spot
- Find a certain spot
- Reset the program

By itself, stepping through code might not be very helpful, except for locating a spot where things go completely awry. But controlled execution gives you a chance to examine the state of the program and its data, such as watching output and variables, as described elsewhere in this chapter.

What is a step?

When you debug a program, the smallest unit of execution is the *line*. That means you can control the rate of debugging to the level of a single line of source code. So, if you string several Pascal statements together on one line, you can't debug those statements individually. On the other hand, you can spread a statement out over multiple lines for debugging purposes, and it will still execute as a single step.

All execution in the debugger, including stepping, tracing, and breaking, is based on lines. The integrated debugger always tells you which line it will execute next by highlighting it with an *execution bar*. The execution bar is a different color from your normal text so you can easily see where you're going.

Stepping is the simplest way to move through your code a little bit at a time. Choosing Run | Step Over or pressing *F8* causes the debugger to execute all the code in the statement indicated by the execution bar, including any procedures or functions it might call, before returning control to you. The execution bar then indicates the next complete statement.

For example, take the simple program shown in Listing 6.1:

Listing 6.1
A simple program to step through

```
program StepTest;

    function Negate(X: Integer): Integer;
    begin
      Negate := -X;
    end;

  var
    I: Integer;

  begin
    for I := 1 to 10 do Writeln(Negate(I));
  end.
```

If you bring up *StepTest* in the edit window and press *F8*, the execution bar moves to the **begin** at the start of the main loop, because that's the first thing to be executed in the program. Pressing *F8* a second time executes **begin** and moves the execution bar down to the **for** statement on the next line. Pressing *F8* now causes the entire **for** loop to execute; the numbers –1 to –10 are printed on the user screen, and the execution bar moves to **end**. Pressing *F8* a final time executes **end**, terminating the program.

Although the function *Negate* is called 10 times, the execution bar never moves through it. Stepping tells the debugger not to show the details of any calls made by a single line. Of course, stepping executed the entire **for** loop at once, so you couldn't see changes as the loop progressed. If you want to see the details of a loop, make this simple change to the main loop of the program in Listing 6.1:

Listing 6.2
Code reformatted for better stepping

```
begin
  for I := 1 to 10 do
    Writeln(Negate(I));
end.
```

Because Pascal statements can span more than one line, this program is exactly equivalent to the earlier version, and the code generated is identical. But because the *Writeln* statement now has its own line, the debugger can treat it separately. Now if you press *F8* repeatedly, you'll find that the execution bar returns to the *Writeln* statement 10 times, once for each time through the loop.

Tracing into code

Tracing into code is very much like stepping through code, with the sole exception that when you come to a statement that calls a procedure or function, tracing into the code steps through the procedures or functions, but stepping returns control to you *after* those subprograms finish.

For example, trace through the code in Listing 6.1: Load the file, then choose Run | Trace Into or press *F7*. The first time you do this, the execution bar moves to **begin** in the main program. Pressing *F7* again moves the bar to the **for** statement. Pressing *F7* now traces into the call to the *Negate* function—the execution bar moves to the **begin** statement in the function block. If you continue to press *F7*, the execution bar steps through the function, then when you execute **end**, returns to the calling statement.

The format of your code affects the behavior of the execution bar when tracing, although not to the degree it does when stepping. With the code formatted as in Listing 6.1, tracing into the **for** statement follows the execution of the *Negate* function 10 times. If you break the **for** statement into two lines, as in Listing 6.2, tracing the **end** of the function returns the execution bar to the line in the main program that will execute next. The first nine times, that's the function call again. The tenth time, the execution bar moves to the program's **end**.

Stepping vs. tracing

Stepping and tracing perform exactly the same action, except when a call occurs to a procedure or function in the line under the execution bar, or when you execute **begin** at the beginning of a program or unit that uses other units.

Units and their initialization sections are explained in Chapter 7, "Borland Pascal units."

Executing **begin** in a program's main **begin..end** block calls the initialization code for any units used by the program, in the order they appear in the program's **uses** clause. In the same way, executing **begin** at the start of a unit's initialization section calls the initialization code for any other units used by that unit. Stepping and tracing work in these cases as you might expect— stepping over **begin** executes all the initializations, returning control at the next statement only after all have finished; tracing traces into the units' initialization code.

Stepping and tracing object methods

If you use objects in your programs, the debugger treats their methods exactly as it would treat ordinary procedures and functions. Stepping over a method call treats the method as a single step, returning control to the debugger after the method completes running. Tracing into a method loads and displays the method's code and traces through its statements.

Stepping and tracing external code

If you link external code into your program using the {**$L** file name} compiler directive, you can step over or trace into that code if the .OBJ file you link in contains debugging information. Borland Pascal won't know anything about the code you're debugging in these modules, but it will show you the appropriate lines in the source code.

The requirements for external code are explained in Chapter 25 of the Language Guide.

You can debug external code written in any language, including C, C++, and assembly language. As long as the code meets all the requirements for external linking and contains full standard debugging information, the IDE's debugger can step or trace through it.

Taking big steps

Sometimes, of course, you don't want to step through *all* your code, just to get to some part that's causing problems. Fortunately, the debugger gives you the ability to step over large amounts of code and regain control at the point where you want to start stepping slowly.

Use Run | Go To Cursor (or the *F4* key) to specify a spot in your program where you want to run, and then stop. (You're telling the debugger you don't want to go step-by-step until you get to a certain point.) Position the cursor at the line where you want to resume debugging control, then press *F4*. Note that you can do this either as a way to start your debugging session or after you've already been stepping and tracing.

Finding a certain spot

The IDE provides two ways to locate a certain spot in your code. The simplest is the Find Procedure command on the Search menu. Find Procedure asks you for the name of a procedure or function, then finds the proper line in the file where that routine is defined. This approach is useful in general editing, of course, but you can also combine it with the ability to run to a certain spot to execute up to the section of code you want to debug.

Navigating backward

Sometimes in the middle of debugging, it's helpful to know how you got where you are. The Call Stack window shows you the sequence of procedure and function calls that brought you to your current state, up to 128 levels deep. Use Debug | Call Stack to bring up the Call Stack window.

The Call Stack window is particularly useful if you accidentally traced into code you wanted to step over. You can move up the call stack to the call you started tracing into by mistake, then choose Run to Cursor to step over the rest of the call.

Starting over

In the middle of a debugging session, you might want to start over from the beginning. Choose the Run | Reset Program command or press *Ctrl+F2*. This resets all debugging, so running, stepping, or tracing begins at the start of the main program.

Watching program output

When stepping or tracing through your program, it's often helpful to be able to look at the program's output, called the *user screen*. In a Windows application, this is quite simple, because the program is already running in a separate window. In DOS, however, it's not quite that easy. Fortunately, Borland Pascal has several ways you can look at your program's user screen.

Swapping screens

At any time during a debugging session, you can move back and forth between the IDE's display and the user screen. To display the user screen, press *Alt+F5*. To return to the IDE, press any key or click the mouse.

The debugger can also swap screens automatically while you step through a program. You can control when swapping takes place using the Display Swapping options in the Debugger dialog box. The default setting is for *smart* swapping, meaning that the user screen is shown only if the executed statement performs screen output or calls a procedure (even if the procedure performs no output). As soon as the output finishes, the screen swaps back to the IDE.

You can also tell the debugger to swap screens for every line, regardless of output, or to not swap screens at all. Swapping screens for every line is useful if your program sends output directly to the screen, which could overwrite the IDE.

The Output window

The DOS IDE provides a window onto the user screen, called the *Output window*. By choosing the Debug | Output menu command, you open (or bring to the front) an active window containing your program's output. You can move or resize this window just as you would an edit window.

Dual monitors

The IDE gives you the option of using a second monitor for debugging purposes. The monitor must be a monochrome display (because it uses different memory than a color display), and you need to start the IDE with the **/D** command-line option. In dual-monitor mode, the IDE's screen appears on the monochrome screen, your program's output appears on the color screen, and no screen swapping occurs.

Examining values

Stepping and tracing through your code can help you find problems in program flow, but you'll usually want to watch what happens to the values of variables while you step. For example, as you step through a **for** loop, it's helpful to know the value of the index variable. The Borland Pascal IDE has two tools to help you examine the contents of your program's variables: the Watches window and the Evaluate and Modify dialog box.

What's an expression?

Both watching and evaluating operate at the level of *expressions*, so it's important to define just what we mean by expression. An expression consists of constants, variables, and data structures combined with operators and most built-in functions. Almost anything you can use as the right side of an assignment statement can be used as a debugging expression. The exact specifications are shown in Table 6.1.

Table 6.1
Elements of debugger
expressions

Expression element	Acceptable values
Constants	All normal types: *Boolean, Byte, Char,* enumerated, *Integer, Longint, Real, Shortint,* string, and *Word.*
Variables	All types, including user-defined
integer-type	Any integer expression within the variable's range bounds
floating-point	Any floating-point or integer expression within the variable's exponent range; excess significant digits are dropped
Char	Any character expression, including printable characters in single quotes, integer expressions typecast to *Char*, and ASCII constants (#*xx*)
Boolean	*True, False*, or any Boolean expression
enumerated	Any compatible enumerated constant or in-range integer expressions typecast to a compatible enumerated type
Pointer	Any compatible pointer or typecast expression; the function *Ptr* with appropriate parameters

Table 6.1: Elements of debugger expressions (continued)

string	Any string constant (text in single quotes); string variables; string expressions consisting of concatenated string constants and variables
set	Any set constant; any compatible set expression using set operators +, −, and *.
Typecasts	Following standard Pascal rules
Operators	All Borland Pascal operators
Built-in functions	All functions legal in constant declarations
Arrays	Borland Pascal arrays *Mem*, *MemL*, and *MemW*

Watching expressions

If you want to keep track of the value of a variable or expression while you step through your code, you can open a *Watches window*. This IDE window shows variables and their values at any given time.

To open the Watches window, choose Window | Watch. The IDE opens an active Watches window with no active entries. If you choose a variable to watch, the IDE automatically opens a Watches window if you haven't already done so.

Adding a watch

To add a variable to the Watches window, you choose Debug | Watch | Add Watch or press *Ctrl+F7*. If the Watches window is the active window, you can add a watch by pressing *Ins*. The debugger opens a dialog box, prompting you to type in a watch expression. The default expression is the word at the cursor in the current edit window. A history list keeps track of expressions you've watched before.

Tracking the current watch

The watch expression most recently added or modified is the *current* watch expression, indicated by a bullet in the left margin. If the Watches window is active, the current watch expression is affected by keystrokes.

Deleting a watch

To delete the current watch expression, choose Debug | Watch | Delete Watch. If the Watches window is active, you can also delete the current watch expression by pressing *Del* or *Ctrl+Y*. To remove all watch expressions, choose Debug | Watch | Remove All Watches.

Editing a watch   To edit a watch expression, either double-click the expression you want to edit or make that expression the current one, then press *Enter* or choose Debug | Watch | Edit Watch. The debugger opens a dialog box much like the one for adding a watch expression, allowing you to edit the current expression. When you choose OK or press *Enter*, the edited expression replaces the original.

Formatting watch expressions   The Watches window enables you to format your watch expressions a number of ways by adding a comma and one or more format specifiers. For example, although integer values normally display in decimal form, you can specify that an expression be displayed as hexadecimal by putting **,H** after it. Table 6.2 shows all the legal format specifiers and their effects.

Table 6.2
Format specifiers for
debugger expressions

Character	Types affected	Function
$, H, or X	integers	**Hexadecimal.** Shows integer values in hexadecimal with the $ prefix, including those in data structures.
C	*Char*, strings	**Character.** Shows special display characters for ASCII 0..31. By default, such characters show as #*xx* values.
D	integers	**Decimal.** Shows integer values in decimal form, including those in data structures.
F*n*	floating point	**Floating point.** Shows *n* significant digits (where *n* is in the range 2..18, and 11 is the default).
*n*M	all	**Memory dump.** Shows *n* bytes starting at the address of the indicated expression. If *n* is not specified, it defaults to the size in bytes of the type of the variable.
		By default, each byte shows as two hex digits. The $, C, D, H, S, and X specifiers can be used with M to change the byte formatting.
P	pointers	**Pointer.** Shows pointers as *seg:ofs* instead of the default *Ptr(seg:ofs)*.

Table 6.2: Format specifiers for debugger expressions (continued)

R	records, objects	**Record**. Shows field names such as (X:1;Y:10;Z:5) instead of (1,10,5).
S	*Char*, strings	**String**. Shows ASCII 0..31 as #*xx*. Use only to modify memory dumps (see nM above).

Evaluating and modifying

In addition to watching variables as your program executes, the debugger has a facility to let you evaluate expressions at any given moment and change the values of variables at run time.

Evaluating expressions

To evaluate an expression, choose Debug | Evaluate/Modify or press *Ctrl+F4*. The debugger displays an Evaluate and Modify dialog box. By default, the word at the cursor position in the current edit window displays highlighted in the Expression field. You can edit that expression, type in another, or choose one from the history list of expressions you evaluated previously.

The current value of the expression in the Expression field shows in the Result field when you press *Enter* or click Evaluate.

The rules for legal expressions are the same for evaluating as they are for watching; all of the rules shown in Table 6.1 apply. The format specifiers in Table 6.2 also work for specifying the display format for evaluated expression results.

Modifying variables

You can change the value of a variable while debugging by using the Evaluate and Modify dialog box. Enter the variable in the Expression field, then type the new value in the New Value field.

Keep these points in mind when you change the values of variables:

- You can only change individual variables, or elements of arrays or records that are not themselves arrays or records.
- Expressions in the New Value field must meet the restrictions for expressions listed in Table 6.1.
- The expression in the New Value field must evaluate to a result that is assignment-compatible with the variable you want to assign it to. A good rule of thumb is that if the assignment

would cause a compile-time or run-time error, it is not a legal modification value.

- You can't directly modify untyped parameters passed into a procedure or function, but you can typecast them and then assign new values.
- Modifying values, and especially pointer values and array indexes, can have undesirable effects and cause you to overwrite other variables and data structures. Be careful.

Using breakpoints

Borland Pascal gives you the ability to set *breakpoints* in your code for debugging purposes. A breakpoint is a designated position in the code where you want the program to stop executing and return control to the debugger. In a sense, a breakpoint works much like the Go to Cursor command, in that the program runs at full speed until it reaches a certain point. The main differences are that you can have multiple breakpoints and breakpoints that don't break all the time.

Setting breakpoints

To set a breakpoint in your code, move the cursor to the line where you want to break. The line needs to contain executable code—it can't be a comment, a blank, or a declaration. Choosing Toggle Breakpoint on the edit window local menu or pressing *Ctrl+F8* sets the line as a breakpoint, which is indicated by highlighting the entire line.

Breakpoints only exist during your debugging session; they aren't saved in your .EXE file.

Now when you run your program from the IDE it will stop whenever it reaches that line, but *before* it executes the line. The line containing the breakpoint shows in the edit window, with the execution bar on it. At that point, you can do any other debugging actions such as stepping, tracing, watching, and evaluating.

Clearing breakpoints

To clear a breakpoint, move the cursor to the line containing the breakpoint and choose Toggle Breakpoint from the edit window local menu or press *Ctrl+F8*.

Modifying breakpoints

The IDE keeps track of all your breakpoints during a debugging session. Rather than making you chase through your source code files looking for your breakpoints, it enables you to maintain all your breakpoints from a single dialog box. Choose View | Breakpoints to bring up the Breakpoints dialog box. From this dialog box, you can set, remove, edit, and view your breakpoints.

The buttons in the Breakpoints dialog box work as follows:

- To add a new breakpoint, highlight a blank line in the list and choose Edit.
- To clear a breakpoint, highlight it and choose Delete.
- To modify an existing breakpoint, highlight it and choose Edit.
- To find a breakpoint in your code, highlight it and choose View.
- To remove all breakpoints, choose Clear All.

Making conditional breakpoints

The breakpoints added by Toggle Breakpoint are unconditional: any time you get to that line, the debugger stops. When you're editing a new or existing breakpoint, however, you have two extra options in the Edit Breakpoint dialog box that let you create *conditional* breakpoints. You can put two kinds of conditions on breakpoints: *pass counts* and *Boolean conditions*.

Counting passes

Setting a pass count on a breakpoint tells the debugger not to break every time it reaches that point, but instead to break only the nth time. That is, if the pass count is 3, the debugger breaks only the third time it reaches that line.

Testing conditions

You can also enter a Boolean expression as a condition for a breakpoint. For example, you might test if a variable falls in a certain range, or if some flag has been set. You can condition your breakpoints to any Boolean expression that follows the guidelines in Table 6.1.

Breaking without breakpoints

Even if you don't set breakpoints, you can still "break" into the debugger when you run your program from the IDE. At any time when your program is running, press *Ctrl+Break*, and the debugger locates the position in the source code where you interrupted the program. As with a breakpoint, you can then step, trace, watch, or evaluate.

7

Borland Pascal units

This chapter explains what a unit is, how you use it, what predefined units are available, how to write your own units, and how to compile them.

What is a unit?

Borland Pascal gives you access to a large number of predefined constants, data types, variables, procedures, and functions. Some are specific to Borland Pascal; others are specific to programming Windows applications. Because they are numerous and you seldom use all of them in one program, they are split into related groups called *units*. You can then use only the units your program needs.

By using units, you can split your program into different parts and compile them separately. A unit is a collection of constants, data types, variables, procedures, and functions that can be shared by several programs. Each unit is almost like a separate Pascal program—it can have a main body that is called before your program starts and does whatever initialization is necessary.

All the declarations in a unit are related to one another. For example, the *Strings* unit contains all the declarations for null-terminated, string-handling routines.

Borland Pascal provides standard units for your use such as *System*, *Crt*, *WinCrt*, and so on. They support your Borland Pascal programs and are all stored in one of three run-time libraries, depending on your target platform:

Library name	Target platform
TURBO.TPL	DOS real mode
TPW.TPL	Windows
TPP.TPL	DOS protected mode

Your program can use any of the procedures or functions in these units; you don't have to write them from scratch yourself.

A unit's structure

A unit's structure is like that of a program, with some significant differences.

```
unit <identifier>;
interface
uses <list of units>;    { Optional }
  { public declarations }
implementation
uses <list of units>;    { Optional }
  { private declarations }
  { implementation of procedures and functions }
begin
  { initialization code }
end.
```

The unit header starts with the reserved word **unit**, followed by the unit's name (an identifier), much the way a program begins. The next item in a unit is the keyword **interface**. This signals the start of the interface section of the unit—the section visible to any other units or programs that use this unit.

A unit can use other units by specifying them in a **uses** clause. The **uses** clause can appear in two places. First, it can appear immediately after the keyword **interface**. In this case, any constants or data types declared in the interfaces of those units can be used in any of the declarations in this unit's interface section.

Second, it can appear immediately after the keyword **implementation**. In this case, any declarations from those units can be used only in the implementation section.

Interface section

The interface portion—the "public" part—of a unit starts at the reserved word **interface**, which appears after the unit header and ends at the reserved word **implementation**. The interface determines what is "visible" (accessible) to any program (or other unit) using that unit.

In the unit interface, you can declare constants, data types, variables, procedures, and functions. As with a program, these sections can be arranged in any order, and they can repeat themselves. For example, your program might have a **var** section followed by a **const** section, and then have another **var** section.

The procedures and functions visible to any program using the unit are declared here, but their actual bodies—their implementations—are found in the implementation section. You won't need to use **forward** declarations and they aren't allowed. The interface section lists all the procedure and function headers; the implementation section contains the coded logic of the procedures and functions.

The bodies of all the regular procedures and functions are held in the implementation section after all the procedure and function headers have been listed in the interface section.

A **uses** clause can appear in the interface section and must immediately follow the keyword **interface**.

Implementation section

A unit's implementation section—the "private" part—starts at the reserved word **implementation**. Everything declared in the interface portion is visible in the implementation: constants, types, variables, procedures, and functions. The implementation can have additional declarations of its own, although these are not visible to any programs using the unit. Also, the program doesn't know they exist and can't reference or call them. However, these hidden items can be (and usually are) used by the "visible" procedures and functions—those routines whose headers appear in the interface section.

A **uses** clause can appear in the implementation and must immediately follow the keyword **implementation**.

The normal procedures and functions declared in the interface—those that are not inline—must reappear in the implementation. The **procedure/function** header that appears in the implementation should either be identical to that which appears in the interface or should be in the short form. For the short form, type the keyword (**procedure** or **function**), followed by the routine's name (identifier). The routine then contains all its local declarations (labels, constants, types, variables, and nested procedures and functions), followed by the main body of the routine itself. Say the following declarations appear in the interface of your unit:

```
procedure ISwap(var V1,V2: Integer);
function IMax(V1,V2: Integer): Integer;
```

The implementation could look like this:

```
procedure ISwap;
var
  Temp: Integer;
begin
    Temp := V1; V1 := V2; V2 := Temp;
end;  { of proc ISwap }
function IMax(V1, V2: Integer): Integer;
begin
  if V1 > V2 then IMax := V1
    else IMax := V2;
end;  { of func IMax }
```

Routines local to the implementation (that is, not declared in the interface section) must have their complete **procedure/function** header intact.

Initialization section

The entire implementation portion of the unit is normally bracketed within the reserved words **implementation** and **end**. If you put the reserved word **begin** before **end** with statements between the two, however, the resulting compound statement, which looks very much like the main body of a program, becomes the **initialization** section of the unit.

Use the initialization section to initialize any data structures (variables) that the unit uses or makes available through the interface section to the program using it. You can use it to open files for the program to use later.

When a program using that unit is executed, the unit's initialization section is called before the program's main body is run. If the program uses more than one unit, each unit's initialization section is called before the program's main body is executed.

How are units used?

The units your program uses are separately compiled and stored as machine code, not Pascal source code; they are not Include files. Even the interface section is stored in the special binary symbol table format that Borland Pascal uses. Certain standard units are stored in a special file (TURBO.TPL, TPW.TPL, or TPP.TPL) and are automatically loaded into memory along with Borland Pascal itself.

As a result, using a unit or several units adds very little time (typically less than a second) to the length of your program's compilation.

In fact, once a unit has been compiled, using it will *save* you time when you recompile. Because the compiler doesn't recompile a unit unless if has changed, or if the implementation section of a unit it depends on has changed, using units in your program will speed the development process.

As stated earlier, to use a specific unit or collection of units, you must place a **uses** clause at the start of your program, followed by a list of the unit names you want to use, separated by commas:

```
program MyProg;
uses thisUnit, thatUnit, theOtherUnit;
```

When the compiler sees this **uses** clause, it adds the interface information in each unit to the symbol table and links the machine code that is the implementation to the program itself.

The ordering of units in the **uses** clause is not important. If *thisUnit* uses *thatUnit* or vice versa, you can declare them in either order, and the compiler determines which unit must be linked into *MyProg* first. In fact, if *thisUnit* uses *thatUnit* but *MyProg* doesn't need to directly call any of the routines in *thatUnit*, you can "hide" the routines in *thatUnit* by omitting it from the **uses** clause:

```
unit thisUnit;
uses thatUnit;
   ⋮
program MyProg;
```

```
uses thisUnit, theOtherUnit;
  :
```

In this example, *thisUnit* can call any of the routines in *thatUnit*, and *MyProg* can call any of the routines in *thisUnit* or *theOtherUnit*. *MyProg* cannot, however, call any of the routines in *thatUnit* because *thatUnit* does not appear in *MyProg's* **uses** clause.

If you don't put a **uses** clause in your program, Borland Pascal links in the *System* standard unit anyway. This unit provides some of the standard Pascal routines and many Borland Pascal-specific routines.

Referencing unit declarations

Once you include a unit in your program, all the constants, data types, variables, procedures, and functions declared in that unit's interface are available to you. For example, suppose the following unit existed:

```
unit MyStuff;
interface
const
  MyValue = 915;
type
  MyStars = (Deneb, Antares, Betelgeuse);
var
  MyWord: string[20];
procedure SetMyWord(Star: MyStars);
function  TheAnswer: Integer;
implementation
  :
end.
```

What you see here is the unit's interface, the portion that is visible to (and used by) your program. Given this, you might write the following program:

```
program TestStuff;
uses WinCrt, MyStuff;
var
  I: Integer;
  AStar: MyStars;
begin
  Writeln(MyValue);
  AStar := Deneb;
  SetMyWord(AStar);
```

```
    Writeln(MyWord);
    I := TheAnswer;
    Writeln(I);
  end.
```

Now that you have included the **uses** *MyStuff* statement in your program, you can refer to all the identifiers declared in the interface section of *MyStuff* (*MyWord, MyValue,* and so on). But consider the following situation:

```
program TestStuff;
uses WinCrt, MyStuff;
const
  MyValue = 22;
var
  I: Integer;
  AStar: MyStars;

function TheAnswer: Integer;
begin
  TheAnswer := -1;
end;

begin
  Writeln(MyValue);
  AStar := Deneb;
  SetMyWord(AStar);
  Writeln(MyWord);
  I := TheAnswer;
  Writeln(I);
end.
```

This program redefines some of the identifiers declared in *MyStuff*. It compiles and runs, but uses its own definitions for *MyValue* and *TheAnswer*, because those were declared more recently than the ones in *MyStuff*.

You can still continue to refer to the identifiers in *MyStuff* by prefacing each one with the identifier *MyStuff* and a period (.). For example, here's yet another version of the earlier program:

```
program TestStuff;
uses WinCrt, MyStuff;
const
  MyValue = 22;
var
  I: Integer;
  AStar: MyStars;
```

```
function TheAnswer: Integer;
begin
  TheAnswer := -1;
end;

begin
  Writeln(MyStuff.MyValue);
  AStar := Deneb;
  SetMyWord(AStar);
  Writeln(MyWord);
  I := MyStuff.TheAnswer;
  Writeln(I);
end.
```

This third program gives you the same answers as the first one, even though you've redefined *MyValue* and *TheAnswer*. Indeed, it would have been perfectly legal to write the first program as follows:

```
program TestStuff;
uses WinCrt, MyStuff;
var
  I: Integer;
  AStar: MyStuff.MyStars;
begin
  Writeln(MyStuff.MyValue);
  AStar := MyStuff.Deneb;
  MyStuff.SetMyWord(AStar);
  Writeln(MyStuff.MyWord);
  I := MyStuff.TheAnswer;
  Writeln(I);
end.
```

You can preface any identifier—constant, data type, variable, or subprogram—with the unit name.

Implementation section uses clause

Borland Pascal allows you to place an optional **uses** clause in a unit's implementation section. If it's present, the **uses** clause must immediately follow the **implementation** keyword, just as a **uses** clause in the interface section must immediately follow the interface keyword.

A **uses** clause in the implementation section lets you further hide the inner details of a unit, because units used in the implementation section aren't visible to users of the unit. It also enables you to construct mutually dependent units.

Because units in Borland Pascal don't need to be strictly hierarchical, you can make circular unit references. To learn more about circular unit references, see Chapter 10 in the *Language Guide*.

The standard units

See Chapter 12 in the Language Guide for information about each unit in the run-time library.
The units in Borland Pascal's run-time libraries are loaded into memory with Borland Pascal; they're always readily available to you. You normally keep the run-time libraries (TURBO.TPL, TPW.TPL, and TPP.TPL) in the same directory as the compilers (TURBO.EXE, BPW.EXE, and BP.EXE).

Writing your own units

If you want to write a unit that has some useful routines and use these routines in your programs, write the unit and save it with the name you specified in the unit header. Borland Pascal saves the file with a .PAS extension just as it does any file created in the Borland Pascal editor. You can have only one unit in a source file.

Compiling your unit

You have two options for compiling your unit. You may

- Compile the unit with Compile | Compile. Instead of creating an .EXE file, Borland Pascal creates a .TPU, .TPW, or .TPP:

Target platform	Unit file extension
DOS real mode	.TPU
Windows	.TPW
DOS protected mode	.TPP

For example, if your unit is named MYUNIT.PAS, it compiles to MYUNIT.TPW when your target platform is Windows.

See the next section to learn how to use the uses statement.
- Use Compile | Make or Compile | Build to compile a program that includes the unit with the **uses** clause. A .TPU, .TPW, or .TPP file is created, depending on your target platform.

Making your unit available to your program

Copy your new .TPU, .TPW, or .TPP file to the unit directory you specified in the Options | Directories dialog box, or use the /**U** command-line option if you're using the command-line compiler.

If you place the unit in the specified unit directory, you can reference the unit even if it's not in the current directory or in the run-time libraries.

Include the **uses** clause in any program you want to use your new unit. For example, if your new unit is named INTLIB.TPW, enter the **uses** clause in your program like this:

```
uses IntLib;
```

To learn about putting your units in the run-time libraries, see page 134.

To find the unit named in a **uses** clause, Borland Pascal checks to see if it is in the run-time library loaded into memory at startup.

If the unit is not in the run-time library, the compiler searches for it on disk, first in the current directory and then in the directories specified as unit directories (Options | Directories). The compiler assumes the name of the file is the unit name with a .TPU, .TPW, or .TPP extension, depending on the target platform.

If you use the Make or Build command, Borland Pascal searches for the source files specified in a **uses** clause in the same order it searches for .TPU, .TPW, or .TPP files. The compiler assumes the source file is the unit name with a .PAS extension.

An example

Let's write a small unit. We'll call it *IntLib* and put in two simple integer routines—a procedure and a function:

```
unit IntLib;

interface
procedure ISwap(var I,J: Integer);
function  IMax(I,J: Integer): Integer;

implementation
procedure ISwap;
var
  Temp: Integer;
begin
  Temp := I; I := J; J := Temp;
end;  { of proc ISwap }
```

```
function IMax;
begin
  if I > J then
    IMax := I
  else IMax := J;
end;  { of func IMax }
end.  { of unit IntLib }
```

Type this unit, save it as the file INTLIB.PAS, then compile it specifying DOS protected mode as the target platform. The resulting unit code file is INTLIB.TPP. Move it to your unit directory or leave it in the same directory as the following program, which uses the unit *IntLib*:

```
program IntTest;
uses IntLib;
var
  A, B: Integer;
begin
  Write('Enter two integer values:  ');
  Readln(A, B);
  ISwap(A, B);
  Writeln('A = ', A, ' B = ', B);
  Writeln('The max is ', IMax(A, B));
end.  { of program IntTest }
```

Units and large programs

So far we've talked about units only as libraries—collections of useful routines to be shared by several programs. Another function of a unit is to break up a large program into modules.

Two aspects of Borland Pascal make this modular unit functionality work:

- Tremendous speed in compiling and linking
- Ability to manage several code files simultaneously, such as a program and several units

Usually a large program is divided into units that each group procedures by their function. For instance, an editor application could be divided into initializing, printing, reading, and writing files, formatting, and so on. Also, there could be a "global" unit, a unit used by all other units. Together with the main program, this global unit could define all global constants, data types, variables, procedures, and functions.

The skeleton of a large editor program might look like this:

```
program Editor;
uses
  WinCrt, Strings,                    { Standard units from TPW.TPL }
  EditGlobals,                              { User-written units }
  EditInit,
  EditPrint,
  EditRead, EditWrite,
  EditFormat;

  { Program's declarations, procedures, and functions }
begin  { main program }
end.   { of program Editor }
```

The units in this program could either be in TPW.TPL, the Windows run-time library, or in their own individual .TPW files. If the latter is true, then Borland Pascal manages your project for you. This means when you recompile program *Editor* using the compiler's built-in make facility, Borland Pascal compares the dates of each .PAS and .TPW file and recompiles any module whose source has been modified.

For more information about managing large programming projects, see page 81 in Chapter 4, "Programming in a DOS IDE."

Another reason to use units in large programs involves code segment limitations. The 8086 (and related) processors limit the size of a given chunk, or segment, of code to 64K. This means the main program and any given segment can't exceed 64K. Borland Pascal handles this by making each unit a separate code segment. Without units, you're limited to 64K of code for your program.

The TPUMOVER utility

Suppose you want to add a well-designed and thoroughly debugged unit to one of the libraries of standard units so it's automatically loaded into memory when you run the compiler. You can do so by using the TPUMOVER.EXE utility.

For details about using TPUMOVER, see the Tools and Utilities Guide.

You can also use TPUMOVER to remove units from the Borland Pascal standard unit library files, reducing the standard unit's size and the amount of memory it takes up when loaded.

As you've seen, it's easy to write your own units. A well-designed, well-implemented unit simplifies program development; you solve the problems only once, not for each new program. Best of all, a unit provides a clean, simple mechanism for writing very large programs.

8

Using pointers

A *pointer* is a reference to data or code in your program. It's literally the address in memory of the item pointed to. Using pointers enables you to write larger and more flexible programs, and it's especially helpful when you start writing object-oriented programs.

This chapter is designed to help you make better use of pointers, whether you're just starting out with Pascal or you've been programming in Pascal for years but never needed pointers before. It covers these topics:

- Why and when to use pointers
- What is a pointer
- How to use pointers
- Managing pointers effectively

Why use pointers?

Sooner or later, every Pascal programmer runs into a situation that requires the use of pointers. You need to use pointers for these reasons:

- If your program handles large amounts of data (more than 64K total)
- If your program uses data of unknown size at compile time
- If your program uses temporary data buffers

- If your program handles multiple data types
- If your program uses linked lists of records or objects

Let's look at each reason to use pointers.

Handling large amounts of data

As programs get larger and more complex and need to handle more data, the 64K area Borland Pascal sets aside for data might not be large enough to hold all the data your program needs. Pointers let you get around this.

Local variables don't go in the data segment, so they don't count against the 64K limit.

When you declare global variables in Borland Pascal, the compiler allocates space for them in an area called the *data segment*. The data segment has a maximum size of 64K, meaning that all your global variables can total only 64K. For many programs, this limit doesn't matter, but there are times when you might need more.

For example, suppose you have a program that requires an array of 400 strings, each of them holding up to 100 characters. That array would take up roughly 40K bytes, which is less than the maximum 64K. An array of this size is not a problem, assuming your other variables fit in the remaining 24K.

But what if you need two such arrays at the same time? That would require about 80K, which won't fit in the 64K data segment. To handle larger amounts of data, you need to use the *heap*. Your program can allocate the 80K on the heap, keeping a pointer as a reference to the location of the data. The pointer takes up only 4 bytes in the data segment.

What is the heap?

The heap is all the memory your operating system makes available that isn't being used by your program code, its data segment, and its stack. You can control the amount of heap space available by using the **$M** compiler directive.

Usually in Borland Pascal you can set aside space on the heap, access it through a pointer, and then release the space again. For details about how to allocate space on the heap for your data, see the section "How do you use pointers?" starting on page 141.

Handling data of unknown size

Some Borland Pascal data items (particularly strings and arrays) need to have their sizes specified at compile time, even though they might not need all the allocated space when the program runs. A simple example would be a program that reads a string from the user, such as the user's name. To store that name in a regular string variable, you would have to set aside enough space to handle the largest possible string, even if the name typed is only a few letters. If you wait to allocate that variable on the heap at run time, you can allocate just the number of bytes needed to hold the actual string data.

This is a trivial example, but in an application with hundreds or thousands of such data items (such as multiple windows or lists read from files), allocating only as much space as needed can mean the difference between running successfully and running out of memory.

Handling temporary data buffers

Pointers and the heap are extremely handy for situations when you need memory allocated temporarily, but don't want to commit that memory for the entire duration of the program. For example, a file editor usually needs a data buffer for every file being edited. Rather than declaring at compilation time that you'll have a certain number of buffers of a certain size always allocated for files, you can allocate only as many as you need at any given time, making memory available for other purposes.

Another common example of temporary memory use is sorting. Usually when you sort a large array of data, you make a copy of the array, sort the copy, and then copy the sorted data back into the original array. This protects the integrity of your data. But it also requires that you have two copies of your data while you're sorting. If you allocate the sorting array on the heap, you can sort it and copy it back into the original, then dispose of the sorting array, freeing that memory for other uses.

Managing multiple data types

One less common use of pointers is to point to variable data structures—that is, records or arrays that might not always have the same structure. For instance, you might have a block of memory set aside to hold a "history list" of different-length string items typed into a data-entry field. To read the history list, a routine would scan through the block looking for individual strings. You could use a simple pointer to indicate where the block begins. In this case, the pointer works much the same way as passing an untyped **var** parameter to a procedure or function—you simply want to tell *where* something is, without specifying *what* it is.

Untyped var parameters are explained in Chapter 9, "Procedures and functions," in the Language Guide.

Linked lists

For an example of using linked lists, see "Managing a linked list," on page 148.

One common use of pointers is to tie together *linked lists* of records. In many simple database-type applications, you can hold data records in arrays or typed files, but sometimes you need something more flexible than an array, which has a fixed size. By allocating dynamic records so that each record has a field that points to the next record, you can construct a list that contains as many elements as you need.

What is a pointer?

A pointer is an address of something in your computer's memory. It could be the address of a variable, a data record, or a procedure or function. Normally, you don't care *where* something resides in memory. You just refer to it by name, and Borland Pascal knows where to look.

That's exactly what happens when you declare a variable. For example, if your program includes the following code, you've told the compiler to set aside an area in memory you'll refer to as *SomeNumber*.

```
var SomeNumber: Integer;
```

You won't need to worry about where *SomeNumber* resides in memory; that's why you gave it a name.

You can find out the memory address of *SomeNumber* using the @ operator. *@SomeNumber* is the address of your integer variable. You can assign that address to a *pointer variable*, which is a variable that holds an address of data or code in memory.

Pointer types

You need a pointer variable to hold a pointer, and to create pointer variables, you must have *pointer types*. The simplest pointer type is a standard type called *Pointer*. A variable of type *Pointer* is a generic (or *untyped*) pointer—that is, it's just an address. It has no information about what kind of thing it points to.

So, to use the same *SomeNumber* example, you can assign its address to a pointer variable:

```
var
    SomeNumber: Integer;
    SomeAddress: Pointer;

begin
    SomeNumber := 17;                           { give SomeNumber a value }
    SomeAddress := @SomeNumber;      { assign the address to SomeAddress }
    SomeAddress := Addr(SomeNumber);  { another way to get the address }
end.
```

Untyped pointers aren't used much in Pascal because they are very limited. They are most useful when the item pointed to will vary, because an untyped pointer is compatible with any other pointer. Typed pointers are much more useful, and they are safer, as you'll see in the next section.

Typed pointers

Usually you'll define pointer types that point to a particular kind of item, such as an integer or a data record. As you'll see shortly, you can take advantage of the fact that a pointer knows what it's pointing to. To define a typed pointer, you declare a new type, defined by a caret (^) followed by any other type identifier. For example, to define a pointer to an *Integer*, you could do this:

```
type PInteger = ^Integer;
```

You can now declare variables of type *PInteger*. If you're not going to use the pointer type often, you can simply declare variables as pointers to an already-defined type. For example, given that you've defined *PInteger* as ^*Integer*, the following variable declarations are equivalent:

```
var
  X: ^Integer;
  Y: PInteger;
```

Dereferencing pointers

So far you've seen how to assign values to pointers, but that's not much use if you can't get the values back. You can treat a typed pointer exactly as if it were a variable of the type it points to by *dereferencing* it. To dereference a pointer, you put a caret (^) after the pointer's identifier.

Listing 8.1 shows some examples of dereferencing pointers:

Listing 8.1
Simple examples of pointer
dereferencing.

```
type PInteger = ^Integer;

var
  SomeNumber: Integer;
  SomeAddress, AnotherAddress: PInteger;

begin
  SomeNumber := 17;                  { assign 17 to SomeNumber }
  SomeAddress := @SomeNumber;  { SomeAddress points to SomeNumber }
  Writeln(SomeNumber);                       { prints 17 }
  Writeln(SomeAddress);        { illegal; can't print pointers }
  Writeln(SomeAddress^);                     { prints 17 }
  AnotherAddress := SomeAddress;   { also points to SomeNumber }
  AnotherAddress^ := 99;           { new value for SomeNumber }
  Writeln(SomeNumber);                       { prints 99 }
end.
```

The most critical lines in Listing 8.1 are these:

```
  AnotherAddress := SomeAddress;   { also points to SomeNumber }
  AnotherAddress^ := 99;           { new value for SomeNumber }
```

If you understand the difference between these two statements, you understand the basics of pointers. The first statement assigns an address to *AnotherAddress*; it tells it where to point. The second statement assigns a new value to the item pointed to by *AnotherAddress*. Figure 8.1 shows graphically how the variables change.

Figure 8.1: Values of the variables after executing assignments

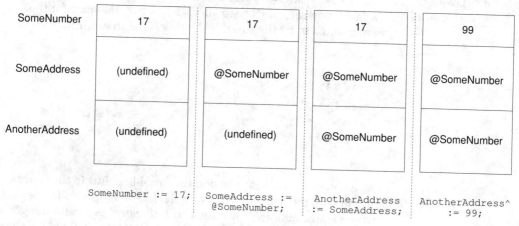

SomeNumber	17	17	17	99
SomeAddress	(undefined)	@SomeNumber	@SomeNumber	@SomeNumber
AnotherAddress	(undefined)	(undefined)	@SomeNumber	@SomeNumber

```
SomeNumber := 17;    SomeAddress :=      AnotherAddress     AnotherAddress^
                     @SomeNumber;        := SomeAddress;        := 99;
```

How do you use pointers?

By now you should have a pretty good idea of the kinds of situations in which you'd use pointers, so it's time to look at how you actually use them. This section covers these topics:

- Allocating dynamic variables
- Deallocating dynamic variables
- Allocating and deallocating specific amounts
- Checking available heap space

Borland Pascal provides two pairs of procedures for allocating and deallocating dynamic variables. *New* and *Dispose* should meet your needs most of the time. *GetMem* and *FreeMem* perform the same jobs, but at a lower level.

Allocating dynamic variables

One of the primary uses of pointers is allocating dynamic variables on the heap. Borland Pascal provides two ways to allocate heap memory to a pointer: the *New* procedure and the *GetMem* procedure.

New is a very simple procedure. Once you've declared a pointer variable, you can call *New* to allocate space on the heap for the item pointed to by the variable. Listing 8.2 is an example:

Listing 8.2
Dynamic variable allocation
with New

```
var
    IntPointer: ^Integer;
    StringPointer: ^String;

begin
    New(IntPointer);                { allocates two bytes on the heap }
    New(StringPointer);             { allocates 256 bytes on the heap }
    ⋮
end.
```

Once you've called *New*, the pointer variable points to the space allocated on the heap. In this example, *IntPointer* points to the two-byte area allocated by *New*, and *IntPointer^* is a valid integer variable (although that integer's value hasn't been defined yet). Similarly, *StringPointer* points to the 256-byte block allocated for a string, and dereferencing it produces a usable string variable.

In addition to allocating memory to a particular dynamic variable, you can use *New* as a function that returns a pointer of a particular type. For example, if *PInteger* is a type defined as *^Integer* and IntPointer is of type *PInteger*, these two statements are equivalent:

```
New(IntPointer);
IntPointer := New(PInteger);
```

This is particularly useful in cases where the pointer variable might need to be assigned items of different types. At times you might want to allocate a dynamic variable without explicitly assigning the resulting pointer to a particular variable. You would probably do this only to create a parameter for a procedure or function:

```
SomeProcedure(New(PointerType));
```

In this case, *SomeProcedure* would probably add the passed pointer to some sort of list. Otherwise the memory allocated would be lost. Borland's *Turbo Vision* and *ObjectWindows* libraries use this technique extensively in assigning dynamic objects to lists.

User's Guide

Using New with objects

Objects and their constructors are explained in Chapter 9, "Object-oriented programming."

Listing 8.3
Constructing dynamic objects

When you use *New* as a function or procedure to allocate a dynamic object, you can add an optional second parameter that specifies the constructor used to initialize the object. For example, in Listing 8.3, the first call to *New* allocates space for an object but doesn't initialize that object in any way. The second call allocates the space and then calls the constructor *Init* to set up the object.

```
type
   PMyObject = ^TMyObject;
   TMyObject = object
      constructor Init;
   end;

var
   MyObject, YourObject: PMyObject;

begin
   New(MyObject);                        { object is not initialized }
   New(YourObject, Init);           { calls Init to initialize object }
end.
```

Deallocating dynamic variables

Variables allocated with *New* must be deallocated when you're finished with them to make the heap space available for other dynamic variables. To deallocate a dynamic variable, you call the *Dispose* procedure. For the example in Listing 8.2, you'd add the following:

```
Dispose(StringPointer);
Dispose(IntPointer);
```

Remember that if you allocate dynamic variables with *New*, you must deallocate them with *Dispose* as soon as you're finished with them.

GetMem and FreeMem

Sometimes you don't want to allocate memory the way *New* does. You might want to allocate more or less memory than *New* allocates by default, or you might not know until run time just how much memory you need to use. Borland Pascal handles such allocations using the *GetMem* procedure.

GetMem takes two parameters: a pointer variable to which you want to allocate memory and a number of bytes to be allocated.

For example, you might have an application that reads 1,000 strings from a file and stores them in dynamic memory. You can't be sure how long any of the strings will be, so you need to declare a string type long enough to accommodate the longest possible string. Assuming that not all the strings take up the maximum length, you have space wasted on unused characters.

To get around this, you could read each string into a buffer, then allocate only enough space to store the actual information in the string. Listing 8.4 shows an example of this:

Listing 8.4
Dynamically allocating string
space

```
type PString = ^String;

var
    ReadBuffer: String;
    LinesRead: array[1..1000] of PString;
    TheFile: Text;
    LineNumber: Integer;

begin
    Assign(TheFile, 'FOO.TXT');
    Reset(TheFile);
    for LineNumber := 1 to 1000 do
    begin
        Readln(ReadBuffer);
        GetMem(LinesRead[LineNumber], Length(ReadBuffer) + 1);
        LinesRead[LineNumber]^ := ReadBuffer;
    end;
end.
```

Instead of allocating 256K for the lines (256 characters per string times 1000 lines), you allocate 4K (4 bytes per pointer times 1000 lines) plus whatever is actually taken up by the text.

Just as you have to dispose of memory allocated with *New*, you need to free the memory you allocate with *GetMem*. The procedure that handles this is called *FreeMem*. Again, just as you pair each call to *New* with a call to *Dispose*, each call to *GetMem* should have a corresponding call to *FreeMem*.

Like *GetMem*, *FreeMem* needs two parameters: the variable to free and the amount of memory to be freed. It is critical that the amount freed be exactly the same as the amount allocated. *New* and *Dispose* always know how many bytes to allocate or free, based on the type of the pointer, but with *GetMem* and *FreeMem* the amount is entirely under your control.

If you free fewer bytes than you allocated, the remaining bytes are lost (a form of heap leak). If you free more bytes than you allocated, you might be releasing memory allocated to another variable, which will probably lead to corrupted data. In protected mode, freeing more memory than you allocated can easily cause a GP fault.

For example, suppose you are going to allocate memory for one or more data records of type *TCheck*, defined in Listing 8.5:

Listing 8.5
A simple record type

```
type
  PCheck = ^TCheck;
  TCheck = record
    Amount: Real;
    Month: 1..12;
    Day: 1..31;
    Year: 1990..2000;
    Payee: string[39];
  end;
```

Each record of type *TCheck* takes up 50 bytes, so if you have a variable *ThisCheck* of type *PCheck*, you could allocate a dynamic check record using this:

```
GetMem(ThisCheck, 50);
```

You could release it later with this:

```
FreeMem(ThisCheck, 50);
```

Using SizeOf with GetMem

Making sure you allocate and free the same amount every time is not enough, however. You also must ensure that you allocate the right amount of memory. Suppose you change the definition of *TCheck*. For example, if you redefined *TCheck.Payee* to be a 50-character string instead of a 39-character string, you would not be getting and freeing enough memory. The safest way to code something like this is to use *SizeOf*:

```
GetMem(ThisCheck, SizeOf(TCheck));
    ⋮
FreeMem(ThisCheck, SizeOf(TCheck));
```

This not only ensures that you allocate and free the same amount, but also guarantees that if you change the size of the type, your code still allocates all the memory you need.

Checking available heap space

Borland Pascal defines two functions that return important information about the heap: *MemAvail* and *MaxAvail*.

MemAvail returns the total number of bytes available for allocation on the heap. Before you allocate a large amount of heap space, it's a good idea to make sure that much space is available.

MaxAvail returns the size of the largest available block of contiguous memory on the heap. When you first run a program, *MaxAvail* is equal to *MemAvail*, because the whole heap is available and contiguous. Once you allocate and free a few blocks, it's likely that the available space on the heap will be *fragmented*, meaning there are blocks of allocated space between the free spaces. *MaxAvail* returns the size of the largest of these free blocks.

The details of how Borland Pascal manages the heap vary depending on the operating system. If you need to know more details, read Chapter 21, "Memory issues," in the *Language Guide*.

Common pointer problems

Pointers enable you to do some important things in Pascal, but there are a couple of common problems you should watch out for when using pointers. The most common pointer problems are these:

■ Dereferencing uninitialized pointers
■ Losing heap memory ("heap leaks")

Dereferencing invalid pointers

One common source of errors with pointers is dereferencing a pointer that hasn't been assigned. Like all Pascal variables, a pointer variable's value is undefined until you assign it a value, so it could point anywhere in memory.

 Always assign values to pointers before using them. If you dereference a pointer that you haven't assigned a value to, the data you read from it could be random bits, and assigning a value to the item pointed to could overwrite other data, your program, or even the operating system. This sounds a little ominous, but with a little discipline it's easy to manage.

To keep from dereferencing pointers that don't point to anything meaningful, you need some way of telling that a pointer is invalid. Pascal provides the reserved word **nil** that you can use as a consistent value for pointers that don't currently point to anything. A **nil** pointer is valid, but unattached. You should check to make sure a pointer is non-**nil** before dereferencing it.

For example, suppose you have a function that returns a pointer to some item in memory. You can indicate that such a function failed to find the item by returning **nil**:

```
var ItemPointer: Pointer;

function FindItem: Pointer;
begin
    ⋮
        { search for item, return pointer to it or nil if not found }
end;

begin
  ItemPointer := nil;                     { start by assuming nil }
  ItemPointer := FindItem;                   { call the function }
  if ItemPointer <> nil then ...  { safe to dereference ItemPointer }
end.
```

☞ Usually it's a good idea to initialize pointers to **nil** if you're not going to assign them some other value right away, then check to make sure such pointers are non-**nil** before dereferencing them.

Losing heap memory

A common problem when using dynamic variables is known as a *heap leak*. A heap leak is a situation where space is allocated on the heap and then lost—for some reason your pointer no longer points to the allocated area, so you can't deallocate the space.

A common cause of heap leaks is reassigning dynamic variables without disposing of previous ones. The simplest case of this is the following:

Listing 8.6
A simple heap leak

```
var IntPointer: ^Integer;

begin
  New(IntPointer);
  New(IntPointer);
end.
```

The first call to *New* allocates eight bytes on the heap and sets *IntPointer* to point to them. The second call to *New* allocates yet another eight bytes, and sets *IntPointer* to point to *them*. Now you have no pointer to the first eight bytes allocated, so there is no way to deallocate them—those eight bytes are lost, as far as this program is concerned.

Of course, a heap leak is usually not as obvious as the one in Listing 8.6. The allocations are almost never consecutive statements, but might be in separate procedures or widely separated portions of the same routine. In any case, the best way to keep track of dynamic variables is to make sure you set them to **nil** when you deallocate them, and then make sure pointer variables are **nil** before you try to allocate them again:

```
var IntPointer: ^Integer;

begin
  New(IntPointer);
    ⋮
  Dispose(IntPointer);
  IntPointer := nil;
    ⋮
  if IntPointer = nil then New(IntPointer);
end.
```

Managing a linked list

Suppose you want to write a program to manage your personal checking account. You can store all the check data in records such as the *TCheck* type defined in Listing 8.5. But it's hard to know when you're writing the program just how many checks you might eventually need to handle. One solution is to create a huge array of check records, but that's a waste of memory. A more elegant and flexible solution is to expand the record definition to include a pointer to a the next record in a list, forming a linked list, as shown in Listing 8.7.

Listing 8.7
A record type for a linked list

```
type
  PCheck = ^TCheck;
  TCheck = record
    Amount: Real;
    Month: 1..12;
    Day: 1..31;
    Year: 1990..2000;
```

```
      Payee: string[39];
      Next: PCheck;                        { points to the next check record }
    end;
```

Now you can read each check record from a file and allocate
space for it. The *Next* field should be **nil** if the record is the end of
the list. Your program needs to keep track of only two pointers:
the first check in the list and the "current" check.

Building the list

Listing 8.8 shows a procedure that builds a linked list of records
read from a file. The code assumes that you've opened a file of
TCheck records called *CheckFile* that contains at least one record.

Listing 8.8
Building a linked list

```
var ListOfChecks, CurrentCheck: PCheck;

procedure ReadChecks;
begin
  New(ListOfChecks);                    { allocate memory for first record }
  Read(CheckFile, ListOfChecks^);                    { read first record }
  CurrentCheck := ListOfChecks;            { make first record current }
  while not Eof(CheckFile) do
  begin
    New(CurrentCheck^.Next);           { allocate memory for next record }
    Read(CheckFile, CurrentCheck^.Next^);           { read next record }
    CurrentCheck := CurrentCheck^.Next;   { make next record current }
  end;
  CurrentCheck^.Next := nil;    { no next record after last one read }
end;
```

Moving through the list

Once you have the list, you can easily search through the list for a
particular record. Listing 8.9 shows a function that locates the first
check with a particular amount and returns a pointer to it.

Listing 8.9
Searching through a linked
list

```
function FindCheckByAmount(AnAmount: Real): PCheck;
var Check: PCheck;
begin
  TempCheck := ListOfChecks;                        { point to first record }
  while (Check^.Amount <> AnAmount) and (Check^.Next <> nil) do
    Check := Check^.Next;
  if Check^.Amount = AnAmount then
    FindCheckByAmount := Check        { return pointer to found record }
  else FindCheckByAmount := nil;            { or nil if none matched }
end;
```

Disposing of the list

When you're through with the list, you go through the items, disposing of each, as shown in the *DisposeChecks* procedure in Listing 8.10.

Listing 8.10
Disposing of a linked list

```pascal
procedure DisposeChecks;
var Temp: PCheck;
begin
  CurrentCheck := ListOfChecks;              { point to first record }
  while CurrentCheck <> nil do
  begin
    Temp := CurrentCheck^.Next;                { store Next pointer }
    Dispose(CurrentCheck);                { dispose of current record }
    CurrentCheck := Temp;                { make stored record current }
  end;
end;
```

Object-oriented programming

Object-oriented programming (OOP) is a method of programming that closely mimics the way all of us get things done. It is a natural evolution from earlier innovations to programming language design: It is more structured than previous attempts at structured programming and more modular and abstract than previous attempts at data abstraction and detail hiding. Three main properties characterize an object-oriented programming language:

- *Encapsulation*: Combining a record with the procedures and functions that manipulate it to form a new data type—an object.
- *Inheritance*: Defining an object and then using it to build a hierarchy of descendant objects, with each descendant inheriting access to all its ancestors' code and data.
- *Polymorphism*: Giving an action one name that is shared up and down an object hierarchy, with each object in the hierarchy implementing the action in a way appropriate to itself.

Borland Pascal's language extensions give you the full power of object-oriented programming: more structure and modularity, more abstraction, and reusability built right into the language. All these features add up to code that is more structured, extensible, and easy to maintain.

The challenge of object-oriented programming is that it requires you to set aside habits and ways of thinking about programming that have been standard for many years. Once you do that, however, OOP is a simple, straightforward, superior tool for solving many of the problems that plague traditional programs.

A note to those of you who have done object-oriented programming in other languages: Put aside your previous impressions of OOP and learn Borland Pascal's object-oriented features on their own terms. OOP is not one single way of programming; it is a continuum of ideas. In its object philosophy, Borland Pascal is more like C++ than Smalltalk. Smalltalk is an interpreter, while from the beginning, Borland Pascal has been a pure native-code compiler. Native-code compilers do things differently (and far more quickly) than interpreters.

And a note to those of you who haven't any notion at all what OOP is about: That's just as well. Too much hype, too much confusion, and too many people talking about something they don't understand have greatly muddied the waters in recent years. Strive to forget what people have told you about OOP. The best way (in fact, the *only* way) to learn anything useful about OOP is to do what you're about to do: Sit down and try it yourself.

Objects?

Yes, objects. Look around you…there's one: the apple you brought in for lunch. Suppose you were going to describe an apple in software terms. The first thing you might be tempted to do is pull it apart: Let *S* represent the area of the skin; let *J* represent the fluid volume of juice it contains; let *F* represent the weight of fruit inside; let *D* represent the number of seeds….

Don't think that way. Think like a painter. You see an apple, and you paint an apple. The picture of an apple is not an apple; it's just a symbol on a flat surface. But it hasn't been abstracted into seven numbers, all standing alone and independent in a data segment somewhere. Its components remain together, in their essential relationships to one another.

Objects model the characteristics and behavior of the elements of the world we live in. They are the ultimate data abstraction so far.

Objects keep all their characteristics and behavior together.

An apple can be pulled apart, but once it's been pulled apart it's not an apple anymore. The relationships of the parts to the whole and to one another are plainer when everything is kept together in one wrapper. This is called *encapsulation*, and it's very important. We'll return to encapsulation in a little while.

Equally important, objects can *inherit* characteristics and behavior from what are called *ancestor objects*. This is an intuitive leap; inheritance is perhaps the single biggest difference between object-oriented Borland Pascal and standard Pascal programming today.

Inheritance

The goal of science is to describe the workings of the universe. Much of the work of science, in furthering that goal, is simply the creation of family trees. When entomologists return from the Amazon with a previously unknown insect in a jar, their fundamental concern is working out where that insect fits into the giant chart upon which the scientific names of all other insects are gathered. There are similar charts of plants, fish, mammals, reptiles, chemical elements, subatomic particles, and external galaxies. They all look like family trees: a single overall category at the top, with an increasing number of categories beneath that single category, fanning out to the limits of diversity.

Within the category *insect*, for example, there are two divisions: insects with visible wings, and insects with hidden wings or no wings at all. Under winged insects is a larger number of categories: moths, butterflies, flies, and so on. Each category has numerous subcategories, and beneath those subcategories are even more subcategories (see Figure 9.1).

This classification process is called *taxonomy*. It's a good starting metaphor for the inheritance mechanism of object-oriented programming.

The questions a scientist asks in trying to classify a new animal or object are these: *How is it similar to the others of its general class? How is it different?* Each different class has a set of behaviors and characteristics that define it. A scientist begins at the top of a specimen's family tree and starts descending the branches, asking those questions along the way. The highest levels are the most general, and the questions the simplest: Wings or no wings? Each level is more specific than the one before it, and less general. Eventually the scientist gets to the point of counting hairs on the third segment of the insect's hind legs—specific indeed.

Figure 9.1
A partial taxonomy chart of
insects

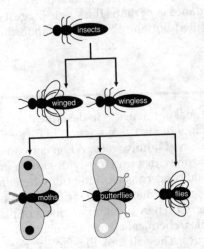

The important point to remember is that once a characteristic is defined, all the categories *beneath* that definition *include* that characteristic. So once you identify an insect as a member of the order *diptera* (flies), you needn't make the point that a fly has one pair of wings. The species of insect called *flies* inherits that characteristic.

As you'll learn shortly, object-oriented programming is the process of building family trees for data structures. One of the important things object-oriented programming adds to traditional languages like Pascal is a mechanism by which data types inherit characteristics from simpler, more general types. This mechanism is inheritance.

Objects: records that inherit

In Pascal terms, an object is very much like a record, which is a wrapper for joining several related elements of data together under one name. Suppose you want to develop a payroll program that produces a report showing how much each employee is paid each payday. You might lay out a record like this:

We start all our type names with the letter T. This is a convention you may want to follow.

```
TEmployee = record
  Name: string[25];
  Title: string[25];
  Rate: Real;
end;
```

TEmployee is a *record type*; that is, it's a template that the compiler uses to create record variables. A variable of type *TEmployee* is an instance of type *TEmployee*. The term *instance* is used now and then in Pascal circles, but it is used all the time by OOP people, and you'll do well to start thinking in terms of types and instances of those types.

With type *TEmployee* you have it both ways: You can think of the *Name*, *Title*, and *Rate* fields separately, or when you need to think of the fields working together to describe a particular worker, you can think of them collectively as *TEmployee*.

Suppose you have several types of employees working in your company. Some are paid hourly, some are salaried, some are commissioned, and so on. Your payroll program needs to accommodate all these types. You might develop a different record type for each type of employee. For example, to figure out how much an hourly employee is paid, you need to know how many hours the employee worked. You could design a *THourly* record like this:

```
THourly = record
  Name: string[25];
  Title: string[25];
  Rate: Real;
  Time: Integer;
end;
```

You might also be a little more clever and retain record type *TEmployee* by creating a field of type *TEmployee* within type *THourly*:

```
THourly = record
  Worker: TEmployee;
  Time: Integer;
end;
```

This works, and Pascal programmers do it all the time. One thing this method doesn't do is force you to think about the nature of what you're manipulating in your software. You need to ask questions like, "How does an hourly employee differ from other employees?" The answer is this: An hourly employee is an employee who is paid for the number of hours the employee works. Think back on the first part of that statement: An *hourly* employee is an *employee*....

There you have it!

An *hourly* employee record must have all the fields that exist in the *employee* record. Type *THourly* is a descendant type of type *TEmployee*. *THourly* inherits everything *TEmployee* has, and adds whatever is new about *THourly* to make *THourly* unique.

This process by which one type inherits the characteristics of another type is called *inheritance*. The inheritor is called a *descendant type*; the type that the descendant type inherits from is an *ancestor type*.

The familiar Pascal record types cannot inherit. Borland Pascal, however, extends the Pascal language to support inheritance. One of these extensions is a new category of data structure, related to records but far more powerful. Data types in this new category are defined with a new reserved word: **object**. An object type can be defined as a complete, standalone type in the fashion of Pascal records, or it can be defined as a descendant of an existing object type by placing the name of the ancestor type in parentheses after the reserved word **object**.

In the payroll example you just looked at, the two related object types would be defined this way:

```
type
  TEmployee = object
    Name: string[25];
    Title: string[25];
    Rate: Real;
  end;

  THourly = object(TEmployee)
    Time: Integer;
  end;
```

Use of parentheses to denote inheritance.

Here, *TEmployee* is the ancestor type, and *THourly* is the descendant type. As you'll see a little later, the process can continue indefinitely: You can define descendants of type *THourly*, and descendants of *THourly*'s descendant type, and so on. A large part of designing an object-oriented application lies in building this *object hierarchy* expressing the family tree of the objects in the application.

All the types eventually inheriting from *TEmployee* are called *TEmployee*'s descendant types, but *THourly* is one of *TEmployee*'s *immediate descendants*. Conversely, *TEmployee* is *THourly*'s *immediate ancestor*. An object type (just like a DOS subdirectory) can have any number of immediate descendants, but only one immediate ancestor.

Objects are closely related to records, as these definitions show. The new reserved word **object** is the most obvious difference, but there are numerous other differences, some of them quite subtle, as you'll see later.

For example, the *Name*, *Title*, and *Rate* fields of *TEmployee* are not explicitly written into type *THourly*, but *THourly* has them anyway, by virtue of inheritance. You can speak about *THourly*'s *Name* value, just as you can speak about *TEmployee*'s *Name* value.

Instances of object types

Instances of object types are declared just as any variables are declared in Pascal, either as static variables or as pointer referents allocated on the heap:

```
type
    PHourly = ^THourly;

var
    StatHourly: THourly;   { Ready to go! }
    DynaHourly: PHourly;   { Must allocate with New before use }
```

An object's fields

You access an object's data fields just as you access the fields of an ordinary record, either through the **with** statement or by *dotting*; for example,

```
AnHourly.Rate := 9.45;

with AnHourly do
begin
    Name  := 'Sanderson, Arthur';
    Title := 'Word processor';
end;
```

Don't forget: An object's inherited fields are not treated specially simply because they are inherited.

Remember that inherited fields are just as accessible as fields declared within a given object type. For example, even though *Name*, *Title*, and *Rate* are not part of *THourly*'s declaration (they are inherited from type *TEmployee*), you can specify them as though they were declared within *THourly*:

```
AnHourly.Name := 'Arthur Sanderson';
```

Good practice and bad practice

Borland Pascal lets you make an object's fields and methods private; for more on this, see page 164.

Even though you can access an object's fields directly, it's not an especially good idea to do so. Object-oriented programming principles require that an object's fields be left alone as much as possible. This restriction might seem arbitrary and rigid at first, but it's part of the big picture of OOP being built in this chapter. In time you'll see the sense behind this new definition of good programming practice, though there's some ground to cover before it all comes together. For now, take it on faith: Avoid accessing object data fields directly.

So—how are object fields accessed? What sets them and reads them?

An object's data fields are what an object knows; its methods are what an object does.

The answer is that an object's *methods* are used to access an object's data fields whenever possible. A *method* is a procedure or function declared *within* an object and tightly bonded to that object.

Methods

Methods are one of object-oriented programming's most striking attributes, and they take some getting used to. Start by harkening back to that fond old necessity of structured programming, initializing data structures. Consider the task of initializing a record with this definition:

```
TEmployee = record
  Name: string[25];
  Title: string[25];
  Rate: Real;
end;
```

Most programmers would use a **with** statement to assign initial values to the *Name*, *Title*, and *Rate* fields:

```
var
  MyEmployee: TEmployee;

with MyEmployee do
begin
  Name := 'Arthur Sanderson';
  Title := 'Word processor';
  Rate := 9.45;
end;
```

This works well, but it's tightly bound to one specific record instance, *MyEmployee*. If more than one *TEmployee* record needs to be initialized, you'll need more **with** statements that do essentially the same thing. The natural next step is to build an initialization procedure that generalizes the **with** statement to encompass any instance of a *TEmployee* type passed as a parameter:

```
procedure InitTEmployee(var Worker: TEmployee; AName,
  ATitle: String; ARate: Real);
begin
  with Worker do
  begin
    Name  := AName;
    Title := ATitle;
    Rate  := ARate;
  end;
end;
```

This does the job, all right—but if you're getting the feeling that it's a little more fooling around than it ought to be, you're feeling the same thing that object-oriented programming's early proponents felt.

It's a feeling that implies that, well, you've designed procedure *InitTEmployee* specifically to serve type *TEmployee*. Why, then, must you keep specifying what record type and instance *InitTEmployee* acts upon? There should be some way to weld together the record type and the code that serves it into one seamless whole.

Now there is: It's called a *method*. A method is a procedure or function welded so tightly to a given type that the method is surrounded by an invisible **with** statement, making instances of that type accessible from within the method. The type definition includes the header of the method. The full definition of the method is qualified with the name of the type. Object type and object method are the two faces of this new species of structure called an object:

```
type
  TEmployee = object
    Name, Title: string[25];
    Rate: Real;
    procedure Init(NewName, NewTitle: string[25];
      NewRate: Real);
  end;
```

```
procedure TEmployee.Init(NewName, NewTitle: string[25]; NewRate:
  Real);
begin
  Name  := NewName;  { The Name field of an TEmployee object }
  Title := NewTitle; { The Title field of an TEmployee object }
  Rate  := NewRate;  { The Rate field of an TEmployee object }
end;
```

Now, to initialize an instance of type *TEmployee*, you simply call its method as though the method were a field of a record, which in one very real sense it is:

```
var
  AnEmployee: TEmployee;

AnEmployee.Init('Sara Adams, Account manager, 15000');  { Easy, no? }
```

Code and data together

One of the most important tenets of object-oriented programming is that the programmer should think of code and data *together* during program design. Neither code nor data exists in a vacuum. Data directs the flow of code, and code manipulates the shape and values of data.

When your data and code are separate entities, there's always the danger of calling the right procedure with the wrong data or the wrong procedure with the right data. Matching the two is the programmer's job, and while Pascal's strong typing does help, at best it can only say what *doesn't* go together.

Pascal says nothing about what *does* go together. If it's not in a comment or in your head, you take your chances.

By bundling code and data declarations together, an object helps keep them in sync. Typically, to get the value of one of an object's fields, you call a method belonging to that object that returns the value of the desired field. To set the value of a field, you call a method that assigns a new value to that field.

For details on how to enforce encapsulation, see "Private section" on page 164. Like many aspects of object-oriented programming, respect for encapsulated data is a discipline you should always observe. It's better to access an object's data by using the methods it provides, instead of reading the data directly. Borland Pascal lets you enforce encapsulation through the use of a **private** declaration in an object's declaration.

Defining methods

The process of defining an object's methods is reminiscent of Borland Pascal units. Inside an object, a method is defined by the header of the function or procedure acting as a method:

```
type
  TEmployee = object
    Name, Title: string[25];
    Rate: Real;
    procedure Init(AName, ATitle: String; ARate: Real);
    function GetName : String
    function GetTitle: String;
    function GetRate : Real;
  end;
```

All data fields must be declared before the first method declaration.

As with procedure and function declarations in a unit's **interface** section, method declarations within an object tell *what* a method does, but not *how*.

The *how* is defined *outside* the object definition, in a separate procedure or function declaration. When methods are fully defined outside the object, the name of the object type that owns the method, followed by a period, must precede the method name:

```
procedure TEmployee.Init(AName, ATitle: String;
  ARate: Real);
begin
  Name  := AName;
  Title := ATitle;
  Rate  := ARate;
end;

function TEmployee.GetName: String;
  GetName := Name;
end;

function TEmployee.GetTitle: String;
begin
  GetTitle := Title;
end;

function TEmployee.GetRate: Real;
begin
  GetRate := Rate;
end;
```

Method definition follows the intuitive dotting method of specifying a record field. In addition to having a definition of *TEmployee.GetName*, it would be completely legal to define a procedure named *GetName* without the identifier *TEmployee* preceding it. However, the "outside" *GetName* would have no connection to the object type *TEmployee* and would probably confuse the sense of the program as well.

Method scope and the Self parameter

Notice that nowhere inside a method is there an explicit `with` `object` `do`... construct. The data fields of an object are freely available to that object's methods. Although they are separated in the source code, the method bodies and the object's data fields really share the same scope.

This is why one of *TEmployee*'s methods can contain the statement `GetTitle := Title` without any qualifier to *Title*. It's because *Title belongs to the object that called the method*. When an object calls a method, there is an implicit statement to the effect `with` `myself` `do` `method` linking the object and its method in scope.

This implicit **with** statement is accomplished by the passing of an invisible parameter to the method each time any method is called. This parameter is called *Self*, and is actually a full 32-bit pointer to the object instance making the method call. The *GetRate* method belonging to *TEmployee* is roughly equivalent to the following:

This example is not fully correct syntactically; it's here to give you a fuller appreciation for the special link between an object and its methods.

```
function TEmployee.GetRate(var Self: TEmployee): Integer;
begin
  GetRate := Self.Rate;
end;
```

Is it important for you to be aware of *Self*? Ordinarily, no: Borland Pascal's generated code handles it automatically in virtually all cases. There are a few circumstances, however, when you might have to intervene inside a method and make explicit use of the *Self* parameter.

For more details on method call stack frames, see Chapter 22 in the Language Guide.

The *Self* parameter is part of the physical stack frame for all method calls. Methods implemented as externals in assembly language must take *Self* into account when they access method parameters on the stack.

Object data fields and method formal parameters

One consequence of the fact that methods and their objects share the same scope is that a method's formal parameters cannot be identical to any of the object's data fields. This is not a new restriction imposed by object-oriented programming, but rather the same old scoping rule that Pascal has always had. It's the same as not allowing the formal parameters of a procedure to be identical to the procedure's local variables:

```
procedure CrunchIt(Crunchee: MyDataRec; Crunchby, ErrorCode:
  Integer);
var
  A, B: Char;
  ErrorCode: Integer; { This declaration causes an error! }
begin
  ⋮
```

A procedure's local variables and its formal parameters share the same scope and thus cannot be identical. You'll get "Error 4: Duplicate identifier" if you try to compile something like this; the same error occurs if you try to give a method a formal parameter identical to any field in the object that owns the method.

The circumstances are a little different, since having procedure headers inside a data structure is a wrinkle new to Borland Pascal, but the guiding principles of Pascal scoping have not changed at all.

Objects exported by units

It makes good sense to define objects in units, with the object type declaration in the interface section of the unit, and the procedure bodies of the object type's methods defined in the implementation section.

By "exported" we mean "defined within the interface section of a unit."

Units can have their own private object type definitions in the implementation section, and such types are subject to the same restrictions as any types defined in a unit implementation section. An object type defined in the interface section of a unit can have descendant object types defined in the implementation section of the unit. In a case where unit *B* uses unit *A*, unit *B* can also define descendant types of any object type exported by unit *A*.

The object types and methods described earlier can be defined within a unit as shown in WORKERS.PAS on your disk. To make use of the object types and methods defined in unit *Workers*, you use the unit in your own program, and declare an instance of type *THourly* in the **var** section of your program:

```
program HourRpt;

uses WinCrt, Workers;

var
   AnHourly: THourly;
   :
```

To create and print the hourly employee's name, title, and amount of pay represented by *AnHourly*, you call *AnHourly*'s methods, using the dot syntax:

```
AnHourly.Init('Sara Adams', 'Account manager', 1400);
                              { Initializes an instance of THourly with }
                              { employee data for Sara Adams }
AnHourly.Show;                { Writes name, title, and pay amount }
```

Objects can also be typed constants.

Objects, being very similar to records, can also be used inside **with** statements. In that case, naming the object that owns the method isn't necessary:

```
with AnHourly do
begin
   Init('Sara Adams', 'Account manager', 1400);
   Show;
end;
```

Just as with records, objects can be passed to procedures as parameters and (as you'll see later on) can also be allocated on the heap.

Private section

In some circumstances you want to export parts of an object declaration. For example, you might want to provide objects for other programmers to use without letting them manipulate the object's data directly. To make it easy for you, Borland Pascal lets you specify private fields and methods within objects.

Private fields and methods are accessible only within the unit in which the object is declared. In the previous example, if the type *THourly* had private fields, they could only be accessed by code within the *THourly* unit. Even though other parts of *THourly* would be exported, the parts declared as private would be inaccessible.

Private fields and methods are declared just after regular fields and methods, following the optional **private** reserved word. Thus, the full syntax for an object declaration is

```
type
NewObject = object (ancestor)
    fields; { these are public }
    methods; { these are public }
private
    fields; { these are private }
    methods; { these are private }
end;
```

Programming in the active voice

Most of what's been said about objects so far has been from a comfortable, Borland Pascal-ish perspective, since that's most likely where you are coming from. This is about to change, as you move on to OOP concepts with fewer precedents in standard Pascal programming. Object-oriented programming has its own particular mindset, due in part to OOP's origins in the (somewhat insular) research community, but also because the concept is truly and radically different.

Object-oriented languages were once called "actor languages" with this metaphor in mind.

One often amusing outgrowth of this is that OOP fanatics anthropomorphize their objects. Data structures are no longer passive buckets that you toss values into. In the new view of things, an object is looked upon as an actor on a stage, with a set of lines (methods) memorized. When you (the director) give the word, the actor recites from the script.

It can be helpful to think of the function *AnHourly.GetPayAmount* as giving an order to object *AnHourly*, saying "Calculate the amount of your pay check." The object is the central concept here. Both the list of methods and the list of data fields contained by the object serve the object. Neither code nor data is boss.

Objects aren't being described as actors on a stage just to be cute. The object-oriented programming paradigm tries very hard to model the components of a problem as components, and not as logical abstractions. The odds and ends that fill our lives, from toasters to telephones to terry towels, all have characteristics (data) and behaviors (methods). A toaster's characteristics might include the voltage it requires, the number of slices it can toast at once, the setting of the light/dark lever, its color, its brand, and so on. Its behaviors include accepting slices of bread, toasting slices of bread, and popping toasted slices back up again.

If you wanted to write a kitchen simulation program, what better way to do it than to model the various appliances as objects, with their characteristics and behaviors encoded into data fields and methods? It's been done, in fact; the very first object-oriented language (Simula-67) was created as a language for writing such simulations.

This is the reason that object-oriented programming is so firmly linked in conventional wisdom to graphics-oriented environments. Objects in Borland Pascal should model components of the problem you're trying to solve. Keep that in mind as you further explore Borland Pascal's object-oriented extensions.

Encapsulation

Declaring fields as private allows you to enforce access to those fields only through methods.

The welding of code and data together into objects is called *encapsulation*. If you're thorough, you can provide enough methods so that a user of the object never has to access its fields directly. Like Smalltalk and other programming languages, Borland Pascal lets you enforce encapsulation through the use of a **private** directive. In this example, we won't specify a **private** section for fields and methods, but instead we will restrict ourselves to using methods in order to access the data we want.

TEmployee and *THourly* are written such that it is completely unnecessary to access any of their internal data fields directly:

```
type
  TEmployee = object
    Name, Title: string[25];
    Rate: Real;
    procedure Init(AName, ATitle: String; ARate: Real);
    function GetName: String;
    function GetTitle: String;
    function GetRate: Real;
    function GetPayAmount: Real;
  end;
```

```
THourly = object (TEmployee)
  Time: Integer;
  procedure Init(AName, ATitle: String; ARate: Real; ATime:
    Integer);
  function GetPayAmount: Real;
end;
```

There are only four data fields here: *Name, Title, Rate,* and *Time.*
The *ShowName* and *ShowTitle* methods print an employee's name
and title respectively. *GetPayAmount* uses *Rate,* and, in the case of
an *THourly* employee, *Time,* to calculate the employee's pay check
amount. There is no further need to access these data fields
directly.

Assuming an instance of type *THourly* called *AnHourly,* you
would use this suite of methods to manipulate *AnHourly*'s data
fields indirectly, like this:

```
with AnHourly do
begin
  Init('Allison Karlon', 'Fork lift operator', 12.95, 62);
  Show;                    { Writes name, title, and pay amount to screen }
end;
```

The object's fields are accessed by the object's methods.

Methods: no downside

Adding these methods bulks up *THourly* a little in source form,
but the Borland Pascal smart linker strips out any method code
that is never called in a program. You therefore shouldn't hang
back from giving an object type a method that might or might not
be used in every program that uses the object type. Unused methods cost you nothing in performance or .EXE file size—if they're
not used, they're simply not there.

About data abstraction

There are powerful advantages to being able to completely
decouple *THourly* from global references. If nothing outside the
object "knows" the representation of its internal data, the programmer who controls the object can alter the details of the
internal data representation—as long as the method headers
remain the same.

Within some object, data might be represented as an array, but
later on (perhaps as the scope of the application grows and its
data volume expands), a binary tree might be recognized as a
more efficient representation. If the object is completely encapsulated, a change in data representation from an array to a binary

tree *does not alter the object's use at all*. The interface to the object remains completely the same, allowing the programmer to fine-tune an object's performance without breaking any code that uses the object.

Extending objects

People who first encounter Pascal often take for granted the flexibility of the standard procedure *Writeln*, which lets a single procedure handle parameters of many different types:

```
Writeln(CharVar);      { Outputs a character value }
Writeln(IntegerVar);   { Outputs an integer value }
Writeln(RealVar);      { Outputs a floating-point value }
```

Unfortunately, standard Pascal has no provision for letting you create equally flexible procedures of your own.

Object-oriented programming solves this problem through inheritance: When a descendant type is defined, the methods of the ancestor type are inherited, but they can also be overridden if desired. To override an inherited method, simply define a new method with the same name as the inherited method, but with a different body and (if necessary) a different set of parameters.

A simple example should make both the process and the implications clear. We have already defined a descendant type to *TEmployee* that represents an employee who is paid hourly wages:

```
const
  PayPeriods = 26;         { per annum }
  OvertimeThreshold = 80;  { per pay period }
  OvertimeFactor = 1.5;    { times normal hourly rate }

type
  THourly = object (TEmployee)
    Time: Integer;
    procedure Init(AName, ATitle: String; ARate: Real; ATime:
        Integer);
    function GetPayAmount: Real;
  end;

procedure THourly.Init(AName, ATitle: String; ARate: Real;
    ATime: Integer);
begin
  TEmployee.Init(AName, ATitle, ARate);
  Time := ATime;
end;
```

```
function THourly.GetPayAmount: Real;
var
   Overtime: Integer;
begin
   Overtime := Time - OvertimeThreshold;
   if Overtime > 0 then
      GetPayAmount := RoundPay(OvertimeThreshold * Rate
         + OverTime * OvertimeFactor * Rate)
   else
      GetPayAmount := RoundPay(Time * Rate);
end;
```

A person who is paid hourly wages is still an employee: That person has everything we used to define the *TEmployee* object (name, title, rate of pay) except the amount of money an hourly employee is paid depends on how many hours that employee works during a pay period. Therefore, *THourly* requires another field, *Time*.

Since *THourly* defines a new field, *Time*, initializing it requires a new *Init* method that initializes *Time* as well as the inherited fields. Rather than directly assigning values to inherited fields like *Name*, *Title* and *Rate*, why not reuse *TEmployee*'s initialization method (illustrated by *THourly.Init*'s first statement)? The syntax for calling an inherited method is *Ancestor.Method*, where *Ancestor* is the type identifier of an ancestral object type, and *Method* is a method identifier of that type.

Calling the method you override is not merely good style; it's possible that *TEmployee.Init* performs some important, hidden initialization. By calling the overridden method, you ensure that the descendant object type includes its ancestor's functionality. In addition, any changes made to the ancestor's method automatically affect all its descendants.

After calling *TEmployee.Init*, *THourly.Init* can perform its own initialization, which in this case consists only of assigning *Time* the value passed in *ATime*.

The *THourly.GetPayAmount* function, which calculates the amount an hourly employee is paid, is another example of an overriding method. In fact, each type of employee object has its own *GetPayAmount* method, because how the employee's pay amount is calculated differs depending on the employee type. The *THourly.GetPayAmount* method must consider how many hours the employee worked, if the employee worked overtime, what the overtime pay factor is, and so on. The *TSalaried.GetPayAmount* method needs only to divide an employee's rate of pay by the number of pay periods per year (26 in our example).

```pascal
unit Workers;

interface

const
  PayPeriods = 26;                  { per annum }
  OvertimeThreshold = 80;           { per pay period }
  OvertimeFactor = 1.5;             { times normal hourly rate }

type
  TEmployee = object
    Name: string[25];
    Title: string[25];
    Rate: Real;
    procedure Init(AName, ATitle: String; ARate: Real);
    function GetName: String;
    function GetTitle: String;
    function GetPayAmount: Real;
  end;

  THourly = object(TEmployee)
    Time: Integer;
    procedure Init(AName, ATitle: String; ARate: Real; ATime:
      Integer);
    function GetPayAmount: Real;
    function GetTime: Integer;
  end;

  TSalaried = object(TEmployee)
    function GetPayAmount: Real;
  end;

  TCommissioned = object(TSalaried)
    Commission: Real;
    SalesAmount: Real;
    procedure Init(AName, ATitle: String; ARate, ACommission,
      ASalesAmount: Real);
    function GetPayAmount: Real;
  end;

implementation

function RoundPay(Wages: Real): Real;
{ Round pay amount to ignore any pay less than 1 penny }
begin
  RoundPay := Trunc(Wages * 100) / 100;
end;
  .
  .
```

TEmployee is at the top of our object hierarchy and it contains the first *GetPayAmount* method.

```
function TEmployee.GetPayAmount: Real;
begin
  RunError(211);          { Give runtime error }
end;
```

You may wonder why all this method does is give you a run-time error. If *TEmployee.GetPayAmount* is called, an error exists in your program. Why? Because *TEmployee* is just the top of our object hierarchy and doesn't define a real worker; therefore, none of the *TEmployee* methods will be called specifically, although they might be inherited. All our employees are hourly, salaried, or commissioned. The *RunTime* error terminates your program and displays "211", the Call to abstract method error message, if your program mistakenly calls *TEmployee.GetPayAmount*.

Next is the *THourly.GetPayAmount* method, which considers such things as overtime pay, the number of hours worked, and so on.

```
function THourly.GetPayAmount: Real;
var
  OverTime: Integer;
begin
  Overtime := Time - OvertimeThreshold;
  if Overtime > 0 then
    GetPayAmount := RoundPay(OvertimeThreshold * Rate +
      OverTime * OvertimeFactor * Rate)
  else
    GetPayAmount := RoundPay(Time * Rate);
end;
```

The *TSalaried.GetPayAmount* method is much simpler; it divides the rate of pay by the number of pay periods.

```
function TSalaried.GetPayAmount: Real;
begin
  GetPayAmount := RoundPay(Rate / PayPeriods);
end;
```

If you look at the *TCommissioned.GetPayAmount* method, you'll see it calls *TSalaried.GetPayAmount*, calculates a commission, and adds it to the amount returned by *TSalaried.GetPayAmount*.

```
function TCommissioned.GetPayAmount: Real;
begin
  GetPayAmount := RoundPay(TSalaried.GetPayAmount + Commission *
    SalesAmount);
end;
```

Important!
☞ Whereas methods can be overridden, data fields cannot. Once you define a data field in an object hierarchy, no descendant type can define a data field with the same identifier.

Inheriting static methods

All the methods shown so far in connection with the *TEmployee*, *THourly*, *TSalaried*, and *TCommissioned* object types are static methods. There is a problem inherent with static methods, however.

To understand the problem, let's leave our payroll example and go back to talking about insects. Suppose you want to build a program that draws different types of flying insects on your screen. You decide to start with a *TWinged* object at the top of your hierarchy. You plan to build new flying-insect object types as descendants of *TWinged*. For example, you might create a *TBee* object type, which differs only from a generic winged insect in that a bee has a stinger and stripes. Of course, a bee has other distinguishing characteristics, but for our example, this is how it might look:

```
type
  TWinged = object(Insect)
    procedure Init(AX, AY: Integer)   { initializes an instance }
    procedure Show;        { displays winged insect on the screen }
    procedure Hide;        { erases the winged insect }
    procedure MoveTo(NewX, NewY: Integer);  { moves winged insect }
  end;

type
  TBee = object(TWinged)
    ⋮
    procedure Init(AX, AY: Integer) { initializes instance of TBee }
    procedure Show;                 { displays a bee on the screen }
    procedure Hide;                 { erases the bee }
    procedure MoveTo(NewX, NewY: Integer;   { moves the bee }
  end;
```

Both *TWinged* and *TBee* have four methods. *TWinged.Init* and *TBee.Init* initialize an instance of their respective objects. The *TWinged.Show* method knows how to draw a winged insect on the screen; the *TBee.Show* methods knows how to draw a TBee on the screen (a winged insect with stripes and a stinger). The *TWinged.Hide* method knows how to erase a winged insect; *TBee.Hide* knows how to erase a bee. The two *Show* methods differ, as do the two *Hide* methods.

The *TWinged.MoveTo* and the *TBee.MoveTo* methods are exactly the same, however. In our example, *X* and *Y* define a location on the screen.

```
procedure TWinged.MoveTo(NewX, NewY: Integer);
begin
  Hide;
  X := NewX;          { new X coordinate on the screen }
  Y := NewY:          { new Y coordinate on the screen }
  Show;
end;

procedure TBee.MoveTo(NewX, NewY: Integer);
begin
  Hide;
  X := NewX;          { new X coordinate on the screen }
  Y := NewY:          { new Y coordinate on the screen }
  Show;
end;
```

Nothing was changed other than to copy the routine and give it *TBee*'s qualifier in front of the *MoveTo* identifier. Since the methods are identical, why bother to put *MoveTo* into *TBee*? After all, *TBee* automatically inherits *MoveTo* from *TWinged*. There seems to be no need to override *TWinged*'s *MoveTo* method, but this is where the problem with static methods appears.

 The term *static* was chosen to describe methods that are not *virtual*. (You will learn about virtual methods shortly.) Virtual methods are in fact the solution to this problem, but in order to understand the solution you must first understand the problem.

The symptoms of the problem are these: Unless a copy of the *MoveTo* method is placed in *TBee*'s scope to override *TWinged*'s *MoveTo*, the method does not work correctly when it is called from an object of type *TBee*. If *TBee* invokes *TWinged*'s *MoveTo* method, what is moved on the screen is a winged insect rather than a bee. Only when *TBee* calls a copy of the *MoveTo* method defined in its own scope are *TBee* objects hidden and drawn by the nested calls to *Show* and *Hide*.

Why? Because of the way the compiler resolves method calls. When the compiler compiles *TBee*'s methods, it first encounters *TWinged.Show* and *TWinged.Hide* and compiles code for both into the code segment. A little later down the file it encounters *TWinged.MoveTo*, which calls both *TWinged.Show* and *TWinged.Hide*. As with any procedure call, the compiler replaces the source code references to *TWinged.Show* and *TWinged.Hide* with the addresses of their generated code in the code segment. Thus, when the code for *TWinged.MoveTo* is called, it calls the code for *TWinged.Show* and *TWinged.Hide*, and everything's in phase.

So far, this scenario is all classic Borland Pascal and would have been true (except for the nomenclature) since Turbo Pascal first appeared on the market in 1983. Things change, however, when you get into inheritance. When *TBee* inherits a method from *TWinged*, *TBee* uses the method exactly as it was compiled.

Look again at what *TBee* would inherit if it inherited *TWinged.MoveTo*:

```
procedure TWinged.MoveTo(NewX, NewY: Integer);
begin
  Hide;        { Calls TWinged.Hide }
  X := NewX;
  Y := NewY;
  Show;        { Calls TWinged.Show }
end;
```

The comments were added to emphasize the fact that when *TBee* calls *TWinged.MoveTo*, it also calls *TWinged.Show* and *TWinged.Hide*, not *TBee.Show* and *TBee.Hide*. *TWinged.Show* draws a winged insect, not a bee. As long as *TWinged.MoveTo* calls *TWinged.Show* and *TWinged.Hide*, *TWinged.MoveTo* can't be inherited. Instead, it must be overridden by a second copy of itself that calls the copies of *Show* and *Hide* defined within its scope; that is, *TBee.Show* and *TBee.Hide*.

The compiler's logic in resolving method calls works like this: When a method is called, the compiler first looks for a method of that name defined within the object type. The *TBee* type defines methods named *Init*, *Show*, *Hide*, and *MoveTo*. If a *TBee* method were to call one of those four methods, the compiler would replace the call with the address of one of *TBee*'s own methods.

If no method by a name is defined within an object type, the compiler goes up to the immediate ancestor type, and looks within that type for a method of the name called. If a method by that name is found, the address of the ancestor's method replaces the name in the descendant's method's source code. If no method by that name is found, the compiler continues up to the next ancestor, looking for the named method. If the compiler hits the very first (top) object type, it issues an error message indicating that no such method is defined.

But when a static inherited method is found and used, you must remember that the method called is the method exactly as it was defined *and compiled* for the ancestor type. If the ancestor's method calls other methods, the methods called are the ancestor's methods, even if the descendant has methods that override the ancestor's methods.

Virtual methods and polymorphism

The methods discussed so far are static methods. They are static for the same reason that static variables are static: The compiler allocates them and resolves all references to them *at compile time*. As you've seen, objects and static methods can be powerful tools for organizing a program's complexity.

Sometimes, however, they are not the best way to handle methods.

Problems like the one described in the previous section are due to the compile-time resolution of method references. The way out is to be dynamic—and resolve such references at run time. Certain special mechanisms must be in place for this to be possible, but Borland Pascal provides those mechanisms in its support of virtual methods.

Important!

Virtual methods implement an extremely powerful tool for generalization called polymorphism. *Polymorphism* is Greek for "many shapes," and it is just that: A way of giving an action one name that is shared up and down an object hierarchy, with each object in the hierarchy implementing the action in a way appropriate to itself.

The simplistic hierarchy of winged insects already described provides a good example of polymorphism in action, implemented through virtual methods.

Each object type in our hierarchy represents a different type of figure onscreen: a winged insect or a bee. Later on, if you were to define objects to represent other types of winged insects such as moths, dragonflies, and so on, you could write a method for each that would display that object onscreen. In the new way of object-oriented thinking, you could say that all these insect types types have in common the ability to show themselves on the screen.

What is different for each object type is the *way* it must show itself to the screen. A bee requires stripes to be drawn on its body, for example. Any winged insect type can be shown, but the mechanism by which each is shown is specific to each type. Yet one word, "Show," is used to display many winged insects. Likewise, if we return to our payroll example, the word "GetPayAmount" calculates the amount of pay for several types of employees.

These are examples of polymorphism. To use polymorphism in Borland Pascal, you use virtual methods.

Early binding vs. late binding

The difference between a static method call and a virtual method call is the difference between a decision made now and a decision delayed. When you code a static method call, you are in essence telling the compiler, "You know what I want. Go call it." Making a virtual method call, on the other hand, is like telling the compiler, "You don't know what I want—yet. When the time comes, ask the instance."

Think of this metaphor in terms of the *MoveTo* problem mentioned in the previous section. A call to *TBee.MoveTo* can go only to one place: the closest implementation of *MoveTo* up the object hierarchy. In that case, *TBee.MoveTo* would still call *TWinged*'s definition of *MoveTo*, since *TWinged* is the closest up the hierarchy from *TBee*. Assuming that no descendant type defined its own *MoveTo* to override *TWinged*'s *MoveTo*, any descendant type of *TWinged* would still call the same implementation of *MoveTo*. The decision can be made at compile time and that's all that needs to be done.

When *MoveTo* calls *Show*, however, it's a different story. Every figure type has its own implementation of *Show*, so which implementation of *Show* is called by *MoveTo* should depend entirely on which object instance originally called *MoveTo*. This is why the call to the *Show* method within the implementation of *MoveTo* must be a delayed decision: When the code for *MoveTo* is compiled, no decision about which *Show* to call can be made. The information isn't available at compile time, so the decision has to be deferred until run time, when the object instance calling *MoveTo* can be queried.

The process by which static method calls are resolved unambiguously to a single method by the compiler at compile time is *early binding*. In early binding, the caller and the callee are connected (bound) at the earliest opportunity, that is, at compile time. With *late binding*, the caller and the callee cannot be bound at compile time, so a mechanism is put into place to bind the two later on, when the call is actually made.

The nature of the mechanism is interesting and subtle, and you'll see how it works a little later.

Object type compatibility

Inheritance somewhat changes Borland Pascal's type compatibility rules. In addition to everything else, a descendant type inherits type compatibility with all its ancestor types. This extended type compatibility takes three forms:

■ Between object instances
■ Between pointers to object instances
■ Between formal and actual parameters

In all three forms, however, it is critical to remember that type compatibility extends *only* from descendant to ancestor. In other words, descendant types can be freely used in place of ancestor types, but not vice versa.

In WORKERS.PAS, *TSalaried* is a descendant of *TEmployee*, and *TCommissioned* is a descendant of *TSalaried*. With this in mind, consider these declarations:

```
type
    PEmployee = ^TEmployee;
    PSalaried = ^TSalaried;
    PCommissioned = ^TCommissioned;

var
    AnEmployee: TEmployee;
    ASalaried: TSalaried;
    ACommissioned: TCommissioned;
    TEmployeePtr: PEmployee;
    TSalariedPtr: PSalaried;
    TCommissionedPtr: PCommissioned;
```

With these declarations, the following assignments are legal:

```
AnEmployee := ASalaried;
ASalaried := ACommissioned;
AnEmployee := ACommissioned;
```

The reverse assignments are not legal.

This is a concept new to Pascal, and it might be a little hard to remember, at first, which way the type compatibility goes. Think of it this way: *The source must be able to completely fill the destination.* Descendant types contain everything their ancestor types contain by virtue of inheritance. Therefore a descendant type is either exactly the same size or (usually) larger than its ancestors, but never smaller. Assigning an ancestor object to a descendant object could leave some of the descendant's fields undefined after the assignment, which is dangerous and therefore illegal.

In an assignment statement, only the fields that the two types have in common are copied from the source to the destination. In the following assignment statement, only the *Name*, *Title*, and *Rate* fields of *ACommissioned* are copied to *AnEmployee*, since *Name*, *Title*, and *Rate* are all that types *TCommissioned* and *TEmployee* have in common.

```
AnEmployee := ACommissioned;
```

Type compatibility also operates between pointers to object types, under the same rule as that applies to instances of object types: Pointers to descendants can be assigned to pointers to ancestors. The following pointer assignments are also legal:

```
TSalariedPtr := TCommissionedPtr;
TEmployeePtr := TSalariedPtr;
TEmployeePtr := TCommissionedPtr;
```

Again, the reverse assignments are not legal.

A formal parameter (either value or **var**) of a given object type can take as an actual parameter an object of its own, or any descendant type. Given the following procedure header, actual parameters could legally be of type *TSalaried* or *TCommissioned*, but not type *TEmployee*.

```
procedure CalcFedTax(Victim: TSalaried);
```

Victim could also be a **var** parameter; the same type-compatibility rule applies.

Warning!
 Keep in mind that there's a drastic difference between a value parameter and a **var** parameter: A **var** parameter is a pointer to the actual object passed as a parameter, whereas a value parameter is only a *copy* of the actual parameter. That copy only includes the fields and methods included in the formal value parameter's type. This means the actual parameter is literally translated to the type of the formal parameter. A **var** parameter is more similar to a typecast, in that the actual parameter remains unaltered.

Similarly, if a formal parameter is a pointer to an object type, the actual parameter can be a pointer to that object type or a pointer to any of that object's descendant types. Given the following procedure header, actual parameters could legally be of type *PSalaried* or *PCommissioned*, but not type *PEmployee*.

```
procedure Worker.Add(AWorker: PSalaried);
```

Polymorphic objects

In reading the previous section, you might have asked yourself: If any descendant type of a parameter's type can be passed in the parameter, how does the user of the parameter know which object type it is receiving? In fact, the user does not know, not directly. The exact type of the actual parameter is unknown at compile time. It could be any one of the object types descended from the **var** parameter type and is thus called a *polymorphic object*.

Now, exactly what are polymorphic objects good for? Primarily this: *Polymorphic objects allow the processing of objects whose type is not known at compile time.* This whole notion is so new to the Pascal way of thinking that an example might not occur to you immediately. (You'll be surprised, in time, at how natural it seems.)

Suppose you've written a toolbox that draws numerous types of winged insects: butterflies, bees, and so on. You want to write a routine that drags insects around the screen with the mouse pointer.

The "old" way would have been to write a separate drag procedure for each type of insect. You would have had to write *DragButterfly*, *DragBee*, and so on. Even if the strong typing of Pascal allowed it (and don't forget, there are always ways to circumvent strong typing), the differences between the types of insects would seem to prevent a general dragging routine from being written.

After all, a bee has stripes and a stinger, a butterfly has large, colorful wings, a dragonfly has iridescent colors, arrgh....

At this point, clever Borland Pascal hackers will step forth and say, do it this way: Pass the winged insect record to procedure *DragIt* as the referent of a generic pointer. Inside *DragIt*, examine a tag field at a fixed offset inside the winged insect record to determine what sort of insect it is, and then branch using a **case** statement:

```
case FigureIDTag of
  TBee        : DragBee;
  TButterfly  : DragButterfly;
  TDragonfly  : DragDragonfly;
  TMosquito   : DragMosquito;
    ⋮
```

Well, placing seventeen small suitcases inside one enormous suitcase is a slight step forward, but what's the real problem with this way of doing things?

What if the user of your toolbox defines some new winged insect type?

For example, what if the user wants to work with Mediterranean fruitflies? Your program does not have a *TFruitfly* type, so *DragIt* would not have a *TFruitfly* label in its **case** statement, and would therefore refuse to drag the new *TFruitfly* figure. If it were presented to *DragIt*, *TFruitfly* would fall out in the **case** statement's **else** clause as an "unrecognized insect."

Plainly, building a toolbox of routines for sale without source code suffers from this problem: The toolbox can work only on data types that it "knows," that is, that are defined by the designers of the toolbox. The user of the toolbox is powerless to extend the function of the toolbox in directions unanticipated by the toolbox designers. What the user buys is what the user gets. Period.

The way out is to use Borland Pascal's extended type compatibility rules for objects and design your application to use polymorphic objects and virtual methods. If a toolbox *DragIt* procedure is set up to work with polymorphic objects, it works with any objects defined within the toolbox—and any descendant objects that you define yourself. If the toolbox object types use virtual methods, the toolbox objects and routines can work with your custom winged-insect figures *on the figures' own terms*. A virtual method you define today is callable by a toolbox .TPU, .TPW, or .TPP unit file that was written and compiled a year ago. Object-oriented programming makes it possible, and virtual methods are the key.

Understanding how virtual methods make such polymorphic method calls possible requires a little background on how virtual methods are declared and used.

Virtual methods

A method is made virtual by following its declaration in the object type with the new reserved word **virtual**. Remember that if you declare a method in an ancestor type **virtual**, all methods of the same name in any descendant must also be declared **virtual** to avoid a compiler error.

Here are the employee objects you have seen in the previous payroll example, properly virtualized:

```
type
  PEmployee = ^TEmployee;
  TEmployee = object
    Name: string[25];
    Title: string[25];
    Rate: Real;
    constructor Init(AName, ATitle: String; ARate: Real);
    function GetPayAmount: Real; virtual;
    function GetName: String;
    function GetTitle: String;
    function GetRate: Real;
    procedure Show; virtual;
  end;

  PHourly = ^THourly;
  THourly = object(TEmployee)
    Time: Integer;
    constructor Init(AName, ATitle: String; ARate: Real; ATime:
      Integer);
    function GetPayAmount: Real; virtual;
    function GetTime: Integer;
  end;

  PSalaried = ^TSalaried;
  TSalaried = object(TEmployee)
    function GetPayAmount: Real; virtual;
  end;
```

```
                           PCommissioned = ^TCommissioned;
                           TCommissioned = object(TSalaried)
                             Commission: Real;
                             SalesAmount: Real;
                             constructor Init(AName, ATitle: String;
                               ARate, ACommission, ASalesAmount: Real);
                             function GetPayAmount: Real; virtual;
                           end;
```

And here is the insect example, complete with virtual methods:

```
               type
                 TWinged = object(Insect)
                   constructor Init(AX, AY: Integer)
                   procedure Show; virtual;
                   procedure Hide; virtual;
                   procedure MoveTo(NewX, NewY: Integer);
                 end;

               type
                 TBee=object(TWinged)
                   constructor Init(AX, AY: Integer)
                   procedure Show; virtual;
                   procedure Hide; virtual;
                 end;
```

Notice first of all that the *MoveTo* method shown of type *TBee* is
gone from *Bee's* type definition. *TBee* no longer needs to override
TWinged's MoveTo method with an unmodified copy compiled
within its own scope. Instead, *MoveTo* can now be inherited from
TWinged, with all *MoveTo's* nested method calls going to *TBee's*
methods rather than *TWinged's*, as happens in an all-static object
hierarchy.

We suggest the use of the
identifier Init for object
constructors.

Also, notice the new reserved word **constructor** replacing the
reserved word **procedure** for *TWinged.Init* and *TBee.Init*. A constructor is a special type of method that does some of the setup
work for the machinery of virtual methods.

Warning!   *Every object type that has virtual methods must have a constructor.*

☞   The constructor must be called before any virtual method is
           called. Calling a virtual method without previously calling the
           constructor can cause system lockup, and the compiler has no
           way to check the order in which methods are called.

☞   Each individual instance of an object must be initialized by a
           separate constructor call. It is not sufficient to initialize one
           instance of an object and then assign that instance to additional
           instances. Although the additional instances might contain correct

User's Guide

data, they are not initialized by the assignment statements and lock up the system if their virtual methods are called, as shown in the following example.

```
var
    FBee, GBee: TBee;                        { create two instances of TBee }

begin
    FBee.Init(5, 9);                          { call constructor for FBee }
    GBee := FBee;                                { GBee is not valid! }
end.
```

What do constructors construct? Every object type has a *virtual method table* (VMT) in the data segment. The VMT contains the object type's size and, for each of its virtual methods, a pointer to the code implementing that method. What the constructor does is establish a link between the instance calling the constructor and the object type's VMT.

That's important to remember: There is only one virtual method table for each object type. Individual instances of an object type (that is, variables of that type) contain a link to the VMT—they do not contain the VMT itself. The constructor sets the value of that link to the VMT—which is why you can launch execution into nowhere by calling a virtual method before calling the constructor.

Range checking virtual method calls

The default state of $R is inactive, {$R-}.

During program development, you might wish to take advantage of a safety net that Borland Pascal places beneath virtual method calls. If the **$R** toggle is in its active state, {**$R+**}, all virtual method calls are checked for the initialization status of the instance making the call. If the instance making the call has not been initialized by its constructor, a range-check, run-time error occurs.

Once you've shaken out a program and are certain that no method calls from uninitialized instances are present, you can speed your code up somewhat by setting the **$R** toggle to its inactive state, {**$R-**}. Method calls from uninitialized instances will no longer be checked for, and will probably lock up your system if they're found.

Once virtual, always virtual

Notice that both *TWinged* and *TBee* have methods named *Show* and *Hide*. All method headers for *Show* and *Hide* are tagged as virtual methods with the reserved word **virtual**. Once an ancestor object type tags a method as **virtual**, all its descendant types that implement a method of that name must tag that method **virtual** as well. In other words, a static method can never override a virtual method. If you try, a compiler error results.

You should also keep in mind that the method heading cannot change in *any* way downward in an object hierarchy once the method is made virtual. You might think of each definition of a virtual method as a gateway to *all* of them. For this reason, the headers for all implementations of the same virtual method must be identical, right down to the number and type of parameters.

This is not the case for static methods; a static method overriding another static method can have different numbers and types of parameters as necessary.

It's a whole new world.

Object extensibility

The important thing to notice about units like WORKERS.PAS is that the object types and methods defined in the unit can be distributed to users in linkable .TPU, .TPW, or .TPP form only, without source code. (Only a listing of the interface portion of the unit need be released.) Using polymorphic objects and virtual methods, the users of the .TPU, .TPW, or .TPP file can still add features to it to suit their needs.

This novel notion of taking someone else's program code and adding functionality to it *without benefit of source code* is called *extensibility*. Extensibility is a natural outgrowth of inheritance: You inherit everything that all your ancestor types have, and then you add what new capability you need. Late binding lets the new meld with the old at run time, so the extension of the existing code is seamless and costs you no more in performance than a quick trip through the virtual method table.

Static or virtual methods

In general, you should make methods virtual. Use static methods only when you want to optimize for speed and memory efficiency. The tradeoff, as you've seen, is in extensibility.

Let's say you are declaring an object named *Ancestor*, and within *Ancestor* you are declaring a method named *Action*. How do you decide if *Action* should be virtual or static? Here's the rule of thumb: Make *Action* virtual if there is a possibility that some future descendant of *Ancestor* will override *Action*, and you want that future code to be accessible to *Ancestor*.

On the other hand, remember that if an object has any virtual methods, a VMT is created for that object type in the data segment and every object instance has a link to the VMT. Every call to a virtual method must pass through the VMT, while static methods are called directly. Though the VMT lookup is very efficient, calling a method that is static is still a little faster than calling a virtual one. And if there are no virtual methods in your object, then there is no VMT in the data segment and—more significantly—no link to the VMT in every object instance.

The added speed and memory efficiency of static methods must be balanced against the flexibility that virtual methods allow: extension of existing code long after that code is compiled. Keep in mind that users of your object type might think of ways to use it that you never dreamed of, which is, after all, the whole point.

Dynamic objects

The use of the word static here does not relate in any way to static methods.

All the object examples shown so far have had static instances of object types that were named in a **var** declaration and allocated in the data segment and on the stack.

```
var
    ASalaried: TSalaried;
```

Objects can be allocated on the heap and manipulated with pointers, just as the closely related record types have always been in Pascal. Borland Pascal includes some powerful extensions to make dynamic allocation and deallocation of objects easier and more efficient.

Objects can be allocated as pointer referents with the *New* procedure:

```
var
    CurrentPay: Real;
    P: ^TSalaried;

New(P);
```

As with record types, *New* allocates enough space on the heap to contain an instance of the pointer's base type, and returns the address of that space in the pointer.

If the dynamic object contains virtual methods, it must then be initialized with a constructor call before any calls are made to its methods:

```
P^.Init('Sara Adams', 'Account manager', 2400);
```

Method calls can then be made normally, using the pointer name and the reference symbol ^ (a caret) in place of the instance name that would be used in a call to a statically allocated object:

```
CurrentPay := P^.GetPayAmount;
```

Allocation and initialization with New

Borland Pascal extends the syntax of *New* to allow a more compact and convenient means of allocating space for an object on the heap and initializing the object with one operation. *New* can now be invoked with two parameters: the pointer name as the first parameter, and the constructor invocation as the second parameter:

```
New(P, Init('Sara Adams', 'Account manager', 2400));
```

When you use this extended syntax for *New*, the constructor *Init* performs the dynamic allocation, using special entry code generated as part of a constructor's compilation. The instance name cannot precede *Init*, since at the time *New* is called, the instance being initialized with *Init* does not yet exist. The compiler identifies the correct *Init* method to call through the type of the pointer passed as the first parameter.

New has also been extended to allow it to act as a function returning a pointer value. The parameter passed to *New* is the *type* of th pointer to the object, rather than the pointer variable itself:

```
type
    PSalaried = ^TSalaried;

var
    P: PSalaried;

P := New(PSalaried);
```

Note that with this version, the function-form extension to *New* applies to *all* data types, not only to object types.

The function form of *New*, like the procedure form, can also take the object type's constructor as a second parameter:

```
P := New(PSalaried, Init('Sara Adams', 'Account manager',
   2400));
```

Fail helps you do error recovery in constructors; see the section "Constructor error recovery" in Chapter 9 of the Language Guide.

A parallel extension to *Dispose* has been defined for Borland Pascal, as fully explained in the following sections.

Disposing of dynamic objects

Just like traditional Pascal records, objects allocated on the heap can be deallocated with *Dispose* when they are no longer needed:

```
Dispose(P);
```

There can be more to getting rid of an unneeded dynamic object than just releasing its heap space, however. An object can contain pointers to dynamic structures or to objects that need to be released or "cleaned up" in a particular order, especially when elaborate dynamic data structures are involved. Whatever needs to be done to clean up a dynamic object in an orderly fashion should be gathered together in a single method so that the object can be eliminated with one method call:

```
MyComplexObject.Done;
```

We suggest the identifier Done for cleanup methods that "close up shop" once an object is no longer needed.

The *Done* method should encapsulate all the details of cleaning up its object and all the data structures and objects nested within it.

It is legal and often useful to define multiple cleanup methods for a given object type. A complex object might need to be cleaned up in different ways depending on how it is allocated or used, or on what mode or state the object is in when it is cleaned up.

Destructors

Borland Pascal provides a special type of method, called a *destructor*, for cleaning up and disposing of dynamically allocated objects. A destructor combines the heap deallocation step with whatever other tasks are necessary for a given object type. As with any method, you can define multiple destructors for a single object type.

Define a destructor along with all the object's other methods in the object type definition:

```
type
  TEmployee = object
    Name: string[25];
    Title: string[25];
    Rate: Real;
    constructor Init(AName, ATitle: String; ARate: Real);
    destructor Done; virtual;
    function GetName: String;
    function GetTitle: String;
    function GetRate: Rate; virtual;
    function GetPayAmount: Real; virtual;
  end;
```

Destructors can be inherited, and they can be static or virtual. Because different shutdown tasks are usually required for different object types, it is a good idea *always* to make destructors virtual, so that in every case the correct destructor is executed for its object type.

Keep in mind that the reserved word **destructor** is not needed for every cleanup method, even if the object type definition contains virtual methods. Destructors really operate only on dynamically allocated objects. In cleaning up a dynamically allocated object, the destructor performs a special service: It guarantees that the correct number of bytes of heap memory are always released. There is, however, no harm in using destructors with statically allocated objects; in fact, by not giving an object type a destructor, you prevent objects of that type from getting the full benefit of Borland Pascal's dynamic memory management.

Destructors really come into their own when polymorphic objects must be cleaned up and their heap allocation released. A polymorphic object is an object assigned to an ancestor type by virtue of Borland Pascal's extended type compatibility rules. An instance of object type *THourly* assigned to a variable of type *TEmployee* is an example of a polymorphic object. These rules govern pointers to objects as well; a pointer to *THourly* can be freely assigned to a pointer to type *TEmployee*, and the referent of that pointer is also a polymorphic object.

The term *polymorphic* is appropriate because the code using the object doesn't know at compile time precisely what type of object is on the end of the string—only that the object is one of a hierarchy of objects descended from the specified type.

The sizes of object types differ, obviously. So when it comes time to clean up a polymorphic object allocated on the heap, how does *Dispose* know how many bytes of heap space to release? No information on the size of the object can be gleaned from a polymorphic object at compile time.

The destructor solves the problem by going to the place where the information *is* stored: in the instance variable's VMT. In every object type's VMT is the size in bytes of the object type. The VMT for any object is available through the invisible *Self* parameter passed to the method on any method call. A destructor is just a special kind of method, and it receives a copy of *Self* on the stack when an object calls it. So while an object might be polymorphic at *compile time*, it is never polymorphic at run time, thanks to late binding.

To perform this late-bound memory deallocation, call the destructor as part of the extended syntax for the *Dispose* procedure:

```
Dispose(P, Done);
```

If you call a destructor outside of a Dispose call, no automatic deallocation occurs.

What happens here is the destructor of the object pointed to by *P* is executed as a normal method call. As the last step, however, the destructor looks up the size of its instance type in the instance's VMT and passes the size to *Dispose*. *Dispose* completes the shutdown by deallocating the correct number of bytes of heap space that previously belonged to *P^*. The number of bytes released is correct whether *P* points to an instance of type *TSalaried* or to one of *TSalaried*'s descendant types, like *TCommissioned*.

Note that the destructor method itself can be empty and still perform this service:

```
destructor AnObject.Done;
begin
end;
```

What performs the useful work in this destructor is not the method body, but instead the epilog code generated by the compiler in response to the reserved word **destructor**. In this respect, the destructor is similar to a unit that exports nothing, but performs some "invisible" service by executing an initialization section before program startup: The action is all behind the scenes.

The WORKLIST.PAS example program that came on your distribution diskettes provides some practice in the use of objects allocated on the heap, including the use of destructors for object deallocation. The program shows how a linked list of worker objects might be created on the heap and then cleaned up using destructor calls when they are no longer required.

Building a linked list of objects requires that each object contain a pointer to the next object in the list. Type *TEmployee* contains no such pointer. The easy way out would be to add a pointer to *TEmployee*, and in doing so ensure that all *TEmployee*'s descendant types also inherit the pointer. However, adding anything to *TEmployee* requires that you have the source code for *TEmployee*, and as said earlier, one advantage of object-oriented programming is the ability to extend existing objects without necessarily being able to recompile them.

The solution that requires no changes to *TEmployee* creates a new object type not descended from *TEmployee*. Type *TStaffList* is a very simple object whose purpose is to head up a list of *TEmployee* objects. Because *TEmployee* contains no pointer to the next object in the list, a simple record type, *TNode*, provides that service. *TNode* is even simpler than *TStaffList*, in that it is not an object, has no methods, and contains no data except a pointer to type *TEmployee* and a pointer to the next node in the list.

TStaffList has a method that lets it add new workers to its linked list of *TNode* records by inserting a new instance of *TNode* immediately after itself, as a referent to its TNodes pointer field. The *Add* method takes a pointer to an *TEmployee* object, rather than an *TEmployee* object itself. Because of Borland Pascal's extended type compatibility, pointers to any type descended from *TEmployee* can also be passed in the *Item* parameter to *TStaffList.Add*.

Program *WorkList* declares a static variable, *Staff*, of type *TStaffList*, and builds a linked list with five nodes. Each node points to a worker object that is one of *TEmployee*'s descendants. The number of bytes of free heap space is reported before any of the dynamic objects is created, and then again after all have been created. Finally, the whole structure, including the five *TNode* records and the five *TEmployee* objects, are cleaned up and removed from the heap with a single destructor call to the static *TStaffList* object, *Staff*.

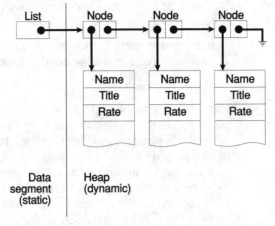

Figure 9.2
Layout of program WorkList's
data structures

Data
segment
(static)

Heap
(dynamic)

Disposing of a complex data structure on the heap

This destructor, *Staff.Done*, is worth a close look. Shutting down a *TStaffList* object involves disposing of three different kinds of structures: the polymorphic worker objects in the list, the *TNode* records that hold the list together, and (if it is allocated on the heap) the *TStaffList* object that heads up the list. The whole process is invoked by a single call to *TStaffList*'s destructor:

```
Staff.Done;
```

The code for the destructor merits examination:

```
destructor TStaffList.Done;
var
  N: TNodePtr;
begin
  while TNodes <> nil do
  begin
    N := TNodes;
    Dispose(N^.Item, Done);
    TNodes := N^.Next;
    Dispose(N);
  end;
end;
```

The list is cleaned up from the list head by the "hand-over-hand" algorithm, metaphorically similar to pulling in the string of a kite: Two pointers, the *TNodes* pointer within *Staff* and a working pointer *N*, alternate their grasp on the list while the first item in the list is disposed of. A dispose call deallocates storage for the first *TEmployee* object in the list (*Item^*); then *TNodes* is advanced

to the next *TNode* record in the list by the statement
`TNodes := N^.Next`; the *TNode* record itself is deallocated; and the process repeats until the list is gone.

The important thing to note in the destructor *Done* is the way the *TEmployee* objects in the list are deallocated:

```
Dispose(N^.Item,Done);
```

Here, *N^.Item* is the first *TEmployee* object in the list, and the *Done* method called is its destructor. Keep in mind that the type of *N^.Item^* is not necessarily *TEmployee*, but could be any descendant type of *TEmployee*. The object being cleaned up is a polymorphic object, and no assumptions can be made about its size or exact type at compile time. In the earlier call to *Dispose*, once *Done* has executed all the statements it contains, the "invisible" epilog code in *Done* looks up the size of the object instance being cleaned up in the object's VMT. *Done* passes that size to *Dispose*, which then releases the exact amount of heap space the polymorphic object occupied.

Remember that polymorphic objects must be cleaned up this way, through a destructor call passed to *Dispose*, if the correct amount of heap space is to be reliably released.

In the example program, *Staff* is declared as a static variable in the data segment. *Staff* could as easily have been itself allocated on the heap, and anchored to reality by a pointer of type *TStaffListPtr*. If the head of the list had been a dynamic object too, the structure would have been disposed of by a destructor call executed within *Dispose*:

```
var
  Staff: TStaffListPtr;
  ⋮
Dispose(Staff, Done);
```

Here, *Dispose* calls the destructor method *Done* to clean up the structure on the heap. Once *Done* is finished, *Dispose* deallocates storage for *Staff*'s referent, removing the head of the list from the heap as well.

WORKLIST.PAS (on your disk) uses the same WORKERS.PAS unit described on page 184. It creates a *List* object heading up a linked list of five polymorphic objects compatible with *TEmployee*, produces a payroll report, and then disposes of the whole dynamic data structure with a single destructor call to *Staff.Done*.

Where to now?

As with any aspect of computer programming, you don't get better at object-oriented programming by reading about it; you get better at it by doing it. Most people, on first exposure to object-oriented programming, are heard to mutter "I don't get it" under their breath. The "Aha!" comes later, when in the midst of putting their own objects in place, the whole concept comes together in the sort of perfect moment we used to call an epiphany. Like the face of woman emerging from a Rorschach inkblot, what was obscure before at once becomes obvious, and from then on it's easy.

The best thing to do for your first object-oriented project is to take the WORKERS.PAS unit (on your disk) and extend it. Once you've had your "Aha!," start building object-oriented concepts into your everyday programming chores. Take some existing utilities you use every day and rethink them in object-oriented terms.

Take another look at your procedure libraries and try to see the objects in them—then rewrite the procedures in object form. You'll find that libraries of objects are much easier to reuse in future projects. Very little of your initial investment in programming effort will ever be wasted. You will rarely have to rewrite an object from scratch. If it will serve as is, use it. If it lacks something, extend it. But if it works well, there's no reason to throw away any of what's there.

Conclusion

Object-oriented programming is a direct response to the complexity of modern applications, complexity that has often made many programmers throw up their hands in despair. Inheritance and encapsulation are extremely effective means for managing complexity. (It's the difference between having ten thousand insects classified in a taxonomy chart, and ten thousand insects all buzzing around your ears.) Far more than structured programming, object-orientation imposes a rational order on software structures that, like a taxonomy chart, imposes order without imposing limits.

Add to that the promise of the extensibility and reusability of existing code, and the whole thing begins to sound almost too good to be true. Impossible, you think?

Hey, this is Borland Pascal. "Impossible" is undefined.

10

Looking into Windows

This chapter is an overview of programming for Microsoft Windows using Borland Pascal, with an emphasis on object-oriented programming. The example presented here uses Object-Windows supplied with Borland Pascal. You'll learn the required behavior of a Windows application, and how object-oriented programming with ObjectWindows automates many tasks and simplifies others.

To get the most out of this chapter, you need to understand object-oriented programming concepts. If object-oriented programming is new to you, study Chapter 9, "Object-oriented programming." You should also know how to use Windows.

What is a Windows application?

Figure 10.1 shows the major components of a Windows application. To understand the topics we'll discuss, you need to be familiar with these components and how they function.

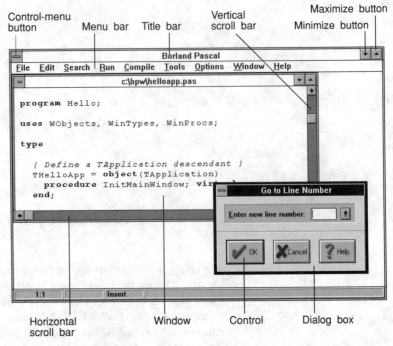

Figure 10.1
The onscreen components of
a Windows application

Control-menu button · Menu bar · Title bar · Vertical scroll bar · Maximize button · Minimize button

Horizontal scroll bar · Window · Control · Dialog box

A Windows application is a special type of PC program that

■ Must be in a special executable (.EXE) file format

■ Runs only with Windows

■ Usually runs in a rectangular window on the screen

■ Follows user-interface guidelines to display and perform in a standard way

■ Can run simultaneously with other Windows and non-Windows applications, including other instances of itself

■ Can communicate and share data with other Windows applications

Benefits of Windows

Windows offers many benefits to both users and developers. Benefits to users include

■ Standard and predictable operation: If you know how to use one Windows application, you know how to use them all.

■ No need to set up devices and drivers for each application: Windows provides drivers to support peripherals.

- Inter-application cooperation and communications.
- Multitasking: the ability to run many applications at once.
- Access to more memory: Windows supports protected mode.

Benefits to developers include

- Device-independent graphics, so graphical applications run on all standard display adapters.
- Immediate support for a wide range of printers, monitors, and mice.
- A rich library of graphics routines.
- More memory for large programs.
- Support for menus, icons, bitmaps, and more.

Requirements

The other side to the array of benefits Windows offers to the user and developer is the more stringent list of hardware requirements. Windows generally requires better graphics, more memory, and faster processors for equivalent performance compared to a DOS application. If you have an 80286 machine or higher and at least 2 MB of memory, Windows runs fine.

Programming facilities

Windows provides a great many programming facilities for the application developer.

An event-driven architecture

Windows is based on an event-driven architecture. This means that all user input is handled as *events*. Whether the event is clicking a mouse button or pressing a keyboard key, an event occurs and Windows generates a *message*. For example, if the user clicks the left mouse button, Windows generates a message called *wm_LButtonDown*. If the user presses a key, Windows generates a *wm_KeyDown* message.

Windows treats all menu and control commands, whether selected by mouse or keyboard, as *wm_Command* messages. This event-driven architecture fits in nicely with Borland Pascal's object-oriented approach.

Device-independent graphics

Windows unifies the process of writing to the screen and printer into a single module, called the graphics device interface (GDI), which provides a common interface to every Windows program. What's more, Windows supplies device drivers for most standard graphics adapters and printers. The resulting system lets you write one application that runs, unmodified, on a large majority of the world's currently available hardware.

Device-independent graphics offers some benefits that might not be immediately apparent. For one, Windows applications are generally easy to install, since they don't have to reconfigure your system with their particular device drivers. Another is that Windows applications often run better on a local area network because each user has his or her own local configuration.

But device-independent graphics comes at a cost. The developer's cost is adhering to the somewhat strict requirements of GDI. GDI limits the programmer's options in designing applications.

Multitasking

Windows lets users run many applications concurrently, eliminating the need for terminate-and-stay-resident (TSR) programs. Not only does Windows allow multitasking, it supports it with a number of facilities for interprocess communication, such as the Clipboard and dynamic data exchange (DDE).

Windows manages multiple applications by limiting each application's use of the full screen to one or more rectangles called *windows*. These windows can be moved, resized, and temporarily hidden as icons, allowing the user to switch between tasks quickly.

From the programmer's side, this means that a program should not write text and graphics directly to screen locations. Instead, it should draw only into its window's *client area*, the area inside the window frame. Likewise, an application has to share the computer's available memory with other applications. A well-behaved Windows application correctly follows Windows rules of screen and memory management.

Memory management

In a typical Windows session, multiple applications are started and closed many times, so it is not feasible to load each application into memory at the end of the previous one: Windows would soon run out of memory. Instead, Windows can *move* most of an application's memory, either to another part of memory or onto disk, to accommodate other applications or Windows itself.

A Windows application, therefore, must accommodate Windows dynamic memory management by avoiding direct access of memory locations. For example, a traditional pointer to a memory location could soon become invalid when Windows reallocates memory, because the pointer might point to a memory location being used for something else.

In place of pointers, Windows applications use *handles*, which are essentially pointers to pointers. Handles are numbers that serve as indexes into a table of pointers managed by Windows. Therefore, Windows applications refer to a window or display context (an area for drawing on the screen) by its handle. There are also handles to application instances, strings, drawing tools, and resources such as menus and icons.

In normal usage, you won't have to deal with memory handles yourself. You can allocate and deallocate heap space using the usual *New*, *Dispose*, *GetMem*, and *FreeMem* routines, and Borland Pascal will deal with Windows to make sure it knows where those pointers actually point.

One of the primary advantages of Windows memory management is the ability to share compiled code among applications. For example, if the user runs two instances of the same application, the two applications use the same compiled code in memory. Likewise, an application can dynamically load a library module that can be shared among different applications. This is known as *a dynamic-link library*, or DLL.

Resources

Resources are descriptions of a Windows application's user-interface devices: its menus, dialog boxes, cursors, icons, bitmaps, strings, and accelerator keys. Windows provides a facility for maintaining these descriptions outside of an application's source code. The application's resources are united with its compiled executable file before the application is run. To limit memory usage, the application calls its resources into memory only when they are needed.

Separating resource specification from the source code has an added benefit: You can alter the look and feel of an application without affecting the program's source code. In fact, you need not even *have* the source code to modify an application's resources. This makes it easy to customize or translate existing Windows applications.

Borland Pascal includes Resource Workshop for creating and customizing resources.

Dynamic linking

Windows allows applications, including Borland Pascal programs, to load and free library modules at run time. These modules must be in a special executable (EXE) format called a *dynamic-link library* (DLL). Often these libraries perform a specific and complex task, such as file-format conversions. When this is the case, an application can use DLLs as filters for file importing and exporting. What's more, DLLs can be shared among a group of applications, promoting reuse and memory conservation.

You can write dynamic-link libraries in Borland Pascal.

Clipboard

The Windows Clipboard lets users transfer information such as text, graphics, and data between applications, between different parts of an application, or to temporary storage for later use. For example, a word-processing application would use the Clipboard for its cut, copy, and paste operations.

Dynamic data exchange

Dynamic data exchange (DDE) is another information transfer protocol. Where the Clipboard is under the user's control, DDE works behind the scenes under the program's control. An application transfers information to another application by sending DDE messages.

Multiple document interface

Multiple document interface (MDI) is a set of user-interface conventions for creating windows that contain child windows inside them. The Borland Pascal Windows IDE is an example of MDI. The user can open several edit windows on the Borland Pascal desktop. Each edit window is a child window.

Figure 10.2
The Borland Pascal Windows
IDE is an MDI application

Windows data types

Because of Windows' data-management scheme and its association with the C programming language, programming for Windows with Borland Pascal is greatly facilitated by some specialized data types. For example, a handle to a window is stored as an *HWnd* type. Borland Pascal and ObjectWindows define new types to accommodate types such as *HWnd*. All these new types and data structures are documented in the *Object-Windows Programming Guide*.

Object-oriented windowing

As you can see, programming for a windowing environment demands an awareness of many events, formats, handles, and other applications, so developing a Windows program can seem like a daunting task. Fortunately, object-oriented programming simplifies the task of programming for a windowing environment, allowing the application developer to focus on the application's function, rather than its form. By using objects to represent complex structures such as windows, a Borland Pascal program can encapsulate its operations and data storage. This is the goal of ObjectWindows.

Object-oriented programming provides a framework within which the programmer uses objects to represent the user-interfac elements of a Windows program. This means that a window is an object.

The ObjectWindows window and application object types manage the message-processing behavior required from a Windows program, greatly simplifying the programmer's interaction with the user. In fact, ObjectWindows objects represent more than just windows: they represent dialog boxes and controls, such as list boxes and buttons.

A better interface to Windows

ObjectWindows uses object-oriented extensions of Borland Pascal to encapsulate the Windows application programming interface (API), insulating you from the details of Windows programming As a result, you can use the Borland Pascal Windows IDE to writ Windows programs with much less time and effort than with approaches that are not object-oriented. Specifically, Object-Windows provides three helpful features: encapsulation of window information, abstraction of Windows API functions, and automatic message response.

Interface objects

While ObjectWindows defines objects for windows, dialog boxes and controls, it supplies only the object's behavior, attributes, and data storage. The physical implementation, the item's visual appearance on the screen, is managed by Windows itself. Thus, ObjectWindows objects, which we'll call *interface objects*, form a partnership with the corresponding visual elements, which we'll call *interface elements*. Successful management of the object/element partnership is the key to successful Windows programming with ObjectWindows.

The connection in the object/element relationship is the window handle. When you construct an interface object, one of the things it does is tell Windows to create an interface element. Windows returns a handle identifying that element, which the object stores in a field called *HWindow*. Many Windows functions require the window handle as a parameter, so storing it in a field keeps it readily accessible to the window object. Similarly, interface object fields can be used to store drawing tools or status information for that particular window.

Abstracting Windows functions

Windows applications control their appearance and behavior by calling Windows functions, the set of almost 600 functions that makes up the Windows application program interface (API). Each function takes a variety of parameters of many different types, which can become quite confusing. Although you can call any Windows function directly from Borland Pascal, ObjectWindows simplifies the task by offering object methods that abstract the function calls.

As noted earlier, many of the parameters for Windows functions are already stored in the fields of interface objects. Thus, methods can use this data to supply Windows functions with parameters. In addition, ObjectWindows groups related function calls into single methods that perform higher-level tasks. The result is a streamlined, easier-to-use API to enhance the existing Windows API.

While this approach greatly reduces your dependence on the hundreds of Windows API functions, it does not restrict you from calling the API directly. ObjectWindows offers the best of both worlds: high-level, object-oriented development plus maximum control over the graphical environment.

Automating message response

In addition to telling the Windows environment to do things, most applications need to be able to respond to the hundreds of Windows messages that result from user actions (such as clicking the mouse), other applications, or other sources. Processing and responding to messages correctly is critical to the proper functioning of your program. After all, your application must respond in *some* way to a menu selection, and responding to any particular message is not hard to do. But writing an application that knows how to respond to nearly 200 different Windows messages can be as intimidating as calling the right Windows functions.

Objects, with their predefined behavior (methods), are perfectly suited to the task of responding to incoming stimuli (Windows messages). ObjectWindows turns Windows messages into

Borland Pascal method calls. Therefore, using ObjectWindows, you simply define a method to respond to each message your application needs to handle. For example, when the user clicks the left mouse button, Windows generates a *wm_LButtonDown* message. If you want a window or control in your program to respond to such mouse clicks, you define a *WMLButtonDown* method keyed to the *wm_LButtonDown* message. Then, when Windows sends that message, your object automatically calls the method you've defined.

Such methods are called *message response methods*. Without object-oriented programming and ObjectWindows, you would have to write a lengthy **case** statement for each window and control to recognize that a message has arrived, sort out what kind of message it is, and finally, decide what to do with it. Object-Windows takes care of all that for you.

The structure of a Windows program

With so many software elements such as DOS, Windows, and applications interacting at once, it helps you to know about how parts of your Windows applications interact with the world around them. This section explores the structure of Windows and typical Windows applications written in Borland Pascal with ObjectWindows.

The structure of Windows

At run time, the functionality of Windows and its API resides in three external library modules called by the currently running applications. Here are the Windows modules:

- KERNEL.EXE handles memory and resource management, scheduling, and interaction with DOS.
- GDI.EXE displays graphics on the screen and printer.
- USER.EXE manages windows, user input, and communications.

These modules are components of the retail version of Windows, so your Windows users already have them on their computers. Programs you supply use these library modules; they don't include them.

Interacting with Windows and DOS

Because of the limited scope of the DOS operating system, it's easy to overlook the contribution DOS makes to the successful operation of your DOS application programs. Nonetheless, a DOS program runs because of the interaction between your application code and the facilities of the operating system.

The same is true of a Windows program. Because Windows offers so many more operating system functions, it is harder to overlook the interplay between Windows and an application. For example, to draw graphics on the screen, your program must call a Windows GDI function. To respond to a user's mouse click, your program must define a message response method. Your program must continually interact with the operating system (DOS plus Windows).

"Hello, Windows"

The traditional way to introduce a new language or environment is to present a "Hello, World" program written in the language or for the environment. This program consists of enough code to display the string "Hello, World" on the screen.

Of course, in Windows there's a lot more to do than that. You need to put up a window, write in it, and then make the window understand how to interact with the world around it, at least enough for you to close the window and make it go away. If you do this from scratch, it takes quite a bit of code just to get those basic tasks done. For example, the program GENERIC.PAS, included on your distribution disks, performs just these minimal tasks, and it's well over 100 lines long!

That's because Windows has a list of requirements an application must meet before it can run in Windows. Even the simplest program requires a substantial amount of code. Fortunately, programs written with ObjectWindows automatically meet most of those requirements, including creating and displaying the main window and storing a handle to the application. Therefore, "Hello, World" is simplified to just 16 lines:

```
program HelloApp;

uses WObjects;

type
  THelloWorld = object(TApplication)
    procedure InitMainWindow; virtual;
  end;

procedure THelloWorld.InitMainWindow;
begin
  MainWindow := New(PWindow, Init(nil, 'Hello, Borland Pascal
world'));
end;

var HelloWorld: THelloWorld;

begin
  HelloWorld.Init('HelloWorld');
  HelloWorld.Run;
  HelloWorld.Done;
end.
```

Application startup responsibilities

An ObjectWindows program's first act upon starting is to take four values from Windows and store them in the following global variables. (This happens automatically, but is something you would have to take care of if you wrote an application that didn't use ObjectWindows).

- *HInstance* stores a handle to the application instance.
- *HPrevInst* stores a handle to the last instance of the same application. It's zero if this is the first instance.
- *CmdShow* stores an integer representing the initial main window display mode. It's used for calls to the *Show* method.
- *CmdLine* stores a string representing the application startup command line, including options and file name such as 'CALC.EXE /M' or 'WORDPROC.EXE LETTER1.DOC'.

As an ObjectWindows application, *HelloApp* must construct and initialize the main window object. It can initialize only the first instance of *HelloApp* with the *InitApplication* method, or it can initialize each instance of *HelloApp* with the *InitInstance* method.

HelloApp starts the message loop by calling *Run*. Finally it ends itself by disposing of the application object using the *Done* method.

Main window responsibilities	The main window of an application is the window that first appears when an application is started. It is responsible for presenting to the user a list of available commands (a menu). During the course of the application session, the main window manages the application's interface, and in many cases, serves as the program's only working area, creating dialog boxes where appropriate. Other, more complex applications might have many windows that serve as work areas. When the user closes the main window, it initiates the process to close the application.

The application development cycle

Because there are certain requirements of any Windows application (initializing the main window, for one), it is usually easiest to begin your application by using an existing Windows application and customizing it. ObjectWindows supplies many sample programs. Choose the one most like your application.

Using the integrated development environment within Windows, you can save a great deal of development time. Because of Windows' multitasking ability, you can run the IDE, Resource Workshop, and your application all at the same time. Not only do the tools supplied with Borland Pascal for Windows make each task easier, but they also cut down on the number of tasks in developing a Windows application. Essentially, the process can be reduced to just these steps:

1. Create the program code and include the file names of the resources the program will use with the {$R filename} directive.
2. Create resources for dialog boxes, menus, and so on.
3. Compile the program.
4. Debug the program interactively.

Learning ObjectWindows

Now that you understand the basics of Windows programming and have been introduced to ObjectWindows, you're ready to program. Begin reading the *ObjectWindows Programming Guide* to learn how to develop an ObjectWindows application step by step.

I N D E X

80286 Code Generation *59*
» (chevron) in dialog boxes *33*
386 enhanced mode, Windows *11*
80x87 emulation *59*
"Borland, contacting *5-6*
→ (arrows) in dialog boxes *32*

A

$A compiler directive *59*
accessing
    additional DOS Help files *42*
    local menus *49*
action buttons *32*
activating
    the DOS ObjectBrowser *65*
    the Windows ObjectBrowser *97*
    a window *30*
active window *29, 30*
adding
    breakpoints *121*
    a program to the Tools menu *75*
    a watch expressions *117*
allocating
    dynamic strings *143*
    dynamic variables *141*
Alternate command set *90*
ancestor *152*
    assigning descendants to *178*
    objects *152*
    types *156*
        immediate *156*
applications
    "Hello, World" *205*
    structure of *204*
    Windows *195*
        developing *207*
        requirements *196, 197*
        startup tasks *206*

arrows (→) in dialog boxes *32*
assembly language, debugging *113*
assigning a keyboard shortcut to a Tools menu
    program *76*
Auto Save option *79*
Auto Track Source option *70, 77*

B

$B compiler directive *59*
background color *50, 92*
    Windows system *93*
backing up distribution disks *7*
binding
    early *176*
    late *177*
BIX, Borland information *5*
block commands *45*
    Borland-style *45, See also* Appendix A in the
    Programmer's Reference
blocks
    behavior of *46, See also* Persistent Blocks
    option
    clearing (deleting) *46*
    copying *46*
    cutting *46*
    pasting *46*
    selecting *45*
    working with *45-47*
boldfacing text in the Windows editor *93*
Boolean Evaluation options *59*
Borland Download BBS *5*
Borland Graphics Interface (BGI)
    EGA palettes and *38*
Borland Pascal
    installing *7*
    starting *26, 35*
        in Windows DOS box *12*
BP.EXE, requirements to run *25*

Ctrl+Break key *122*
CUA command set *90*
current
    directory, how determined *95*
    window *29*
Current Window option *71*
customer assistance *5-6*
customizing the right mouse button *27*
Cut command *46*
Cut to Clipboard button on SpeedBar *85*
cutting blocks of text *46*

D

/D startup option (dual monitors) *36, 115*
data segment *136*
deallocating dynamic variables *141*
Debug Information option *65, 97, 109*
debugging *105-122*
    assembly language *113*
    defined *106*
    dual-monitor *115*
    IFDEF and *63*
    IFNDEF and *63*
    information *109-110*
        defined *109*
        units *109*
    information, how to turn on *109*
    integrated vs. standalone *109*
    object methods *113*
    restarting *114*
    screen swapping *115*
    techniques *107-122*
        overview *107*
    unit initialization code *112*
declaring object instances *157*
default buttons *32*
$DEFINE compiler directive *60*
defining conditional symbols *61*
deleting
    breakpoints *121*
    selected text *46*
    a Tools menu program *76*
    watch expressions *117*
delimiter pair matching *48*
dereferencing pointers *140*
descendant types *156*

desktop
    clearing the *80*
    file *78*
        auto-saving *78*
        defined *79*
        where saved *80*
Desktop Auto Save option *79*
destination, choosing a compile *55*
destructors
    declaring *188*
    defined *187, 188*
    dynamic object disposal *189*
    polymorphic objects and *188*
    static versus virtual *188*
dialog boxes *32-34*
dimmed
    buttons on SpeedBar *85*
    menu commands *27*
directives, compiler *See* compiler, directives
directories, specifying *81*
Directories dialog box *132*
directory
    current work *95*
    unit *132*
display swapping *115*
displaying
    fully qualified identiers *69*
    inheritance information *67*
    reference information *67*
    scope information *67*
Dispose procedure *141*
    extended syntax *187*
distribution disks
    backing up *7*
    defined *8*
documentation, set, books in *1-4*
DoneWinCrt procedure *96*
DOS box *12*
DOS Shell command *40*
DOSPRMPT.PIF file *12*
dotting *157, 162, 164*
DPMI16BI.OVL file *9*
    required for BP.EXE *26, 35*
DPMI, use of extended memory *11*
DPMI conditional symbol *61*
DPMIINST, protected mode and *10*
DPMIMEM environment variable *10*

User's Guia

highlighting text *49-51, 91-93*
  disabling *51*
  selecting files *51*
HInstance global variable *206*
history lists
  clearing *80*
  defined *33*
hot keys *27*
  assigning to Tools menu programs *76*
  on status line *27*
HPrevInst global variable *206*

I

$I compiler directive *59*
I/O Error Checking *59*
IDE
  command-line options *36-39*
  common tasks performed in the *35*
  configuration file *79*
  control characters and *33*
  defined *25*
  DOS
    basic skills *25-34*
    starting *26, 35*
    startup options *36*
  protected-mode (BP.EXE) *25*
    requirements to start *26*
  real-mode (TURBO.EXE) *25*
  Windows (BPW.EXE) *25*
    configuring *104*
    starting the *83*
$IFDEF compiler directive *60, 63*
$IFNDEF compiler directive *60, 63*
$IFOPT compiler directive *60, 63*
IFxxx symbol *62*
immediate ancestors and descendants *156*
implementation section *125*
  procedure/function headers in *125*
  uses clauses in *130*
Include file *56*
incremental search *34*
  in the ObjectBrowser *67*
inheritance *151, 153, 154, 156*
  information, displaying *67*
input boxes *33*
INSTALL program *7*

installing
  additional (DOS) Help files *42*
  Borland Pascal *7*
    disk space requirements *8*
    LCD screens and *12*
instances *155*
  dynamic object *185-192*
  object
    declaring *157*
    linked lists of *190*
  static object *154-185*
integrated debugger *105-122*
Integrated option *109*
interface
  objects *202*
  section of a unit *125*
italicizing text in the Windows editor *93*

J

jumping to a line number *49*

K

KERNEL.EXE *204*
keyboard
  choosing buttons with *32*
  choosing commands with *26*
  shortcut, assigning to Tools menu program *76*

L

/L startup option (LCD screen) *38*
late binding *177*
LCD screens
  installing Borland Pascal for *12*
  running the IDE on *38*
line
  number
    in a window *29*
    jumping to a *49*
  references, editing *70*
linked lists *138, 190*
  using *148-150*
Linker Options dialog box *58*
List (Window menu) command *31*
list all line references *99*
list boxes *34*

User's Guide